THE DARK

Selected Writings of
Brendan Hughes

THE DARK

Selected Writings of
Brendan Hughes

Edited & Introduced by
Róisín Dubh

ISKRA
BOOKS

Published by *Iskra Books* 2023

ISKRA BOOKS
Madison, Wisconsin
U.S. | U.K.
Iskra Books is an independent scholarly publisher—publishing original
works of revolutionary theory, history, education, and art, as well as edited
collections, new translations, and critical republications of older works.

ISBN-13: 978-1-0881-3166-4

British Library Cataloguing in Publication Data
A catalogue record for this book is available from the British Library

Library of Congress Cataloguing-in-Publication Data
A catalog record for this book is available from the Library of Congress

Cover and Interior Art by Ben Stahnke
Typesetting by Róisín Dubh and Ben Stahnke

The Hughes family would like to thank everyone involved in putting Brendan's writings together in one publication. It's hard to believe 2023 marks the 15th anniversary of Brendan's passing. As time has moved on, our memories of him are still very much alive.

We remember Brendan's honesty, integrity, empathy, and—of course—his humour. Although we miss him dearly, the legacy he left helps us all through the difficult times. It's a legacy we've seen grow over the years and we hope future generations can look back on Brendan's life and use his experience as a rallying call for the working class.

CONTENTS

EDITOR'S PREFACE

Róisín Dubh...i

SELECTED ESSAYS FROM IRISH REPUBLICANS

Essay by Anthony McIntyre—April 2023.......................................2

Essay by Dixie Elliott—April 2023...6

Essay by John Nixon—April 2023...8

Essay by Pádraic Mac Coitir—March 2023.................................14

SELECTED ESSAYS AND WORDS FROM BRENDAN HUGHES

Letter to Terry Hughes 1—1 November 1980...............................20

Letter to Terry Hughes 2—5 August 1981...................................22

Interview with Brendan Hughes—Spring 2000...........................24

Radio Free Eireann Interview with Brendan Hughes—Spring 2000.....29

Does Anyone Care?—Autumn 2000...55

So Why Did We Strike?—8 October 2000...................................57

Dances with Buffalos—Winter 2000..60

Interview with Brendan (Darkie) Hughes—4 November 2000............62

Ireland: "A Betrayal of What We Fought For"—December 2000..........68

Hughes No Longer Toes the Provo Line—17 December 2000.............72

On the 20ᵗʰ Anniversary of the Hunger Strike—25 January 2001.....79

What of the Working People?—Spring 2001................................87

Telling Ronnie Flanagan First—27 March 2001 90

The Real Meaning of G.F.A.—8 October 2001 92

Under the Foot of the Mountain—Winter 2022 95

Who Are the Terrorists?—17 January 2002 97

Off with their Beards—17 January 2002 99

Who is Still Here?—22 January 2002 101

They Think It's All Over—4 February 2002 103

Hitler Speaking Hebrew—7 April 2002 105

Trust Your Leaders?—8 April 2002 108

Who Guards the Guards?—10 April 2002 111

The Putrid Smell of the Middle Class—18 April 2002 113

The Terrifying Power of Life and Death—7 June 2002 115

Charlie Hughes and the Courage of the Brave—10 September 2002 117

Palestine & Iraq—16 September 2002 122

Volunteer Patricia McKay—8 May 2003 124

Cheats—11 May 2003 126

No More Lies—3 May 2004 128

Our Fenian Dead—29 January 2006 131

Provos Thrown on the Scrap Heap of History—16 April 2006 133

O'Rawe Told Me His Concerns—19 May 2006 140

Not the IRA Way—13 July 2006 141

Hunger Striker in Fight for Sight—October 2006 143

Sinn Féin Trying to Smear "Dissenters"—3 January 2007 147

AFTERWORD

25 Years of Got Fuck All—Essay by D. Óg—April 2023 150

EDITOR'S PREFACE

Róisín Dubh

April 2023 marked the 25th anniversary of the signing of the *Good Friday Agreement* (GFA)—a significant, so-called peace deal between the major political parties in the North of Ireland. While the mainstream media celebrated this anniversary, with U.S. president Joe Biden having visited the country for the occasion, this sentiment was not shared—and in fact resisted—by many Republican veterans both at home and abroad. This volume is a remembrance of those resistors; of those Irish Republican Army (IRA) veterans who sacrificed it all for a free and united Ireland; of those who continued to speak out against the GFA, even when it became highly unpopular to do so.

According to the sentiments of many Republican veterans, some of whom you will read in this book, the GFA failed in many regards: failing to bring change to the occupied six counties; failing to make better the real conditions of the working class in those counties still occupied by British forces, where Irish language and culture continue to be suppressed—where Republicans are still targeted and harassed by the British courts.

Brendan Hughes (1948 - 2008), one of the most vocal and stalwart of the veterans *critical* of the failures of the GFA, is not a person many might think of as a great theoretician of Republican socialism. He was, however, and by virtue of his working class politics put into direct, transformative practice, an example of a *real* revolutionary thinker, whose writings and ideas showcased lessons learned and what he believed *needed to be done* in the Irish political context. Like much of the working class, Hughes "carried around the hidden injuries of class."[1] Those injuries gave Hughes an unceasing drive to fight for justice and freedom, against injustice and oppression, for a truly socialist Ireland.

Hughes grew up in Belfast, born to a large Catholic family living in a Protestant area. Despite this unique geographical arrangement, Hughes came from a family with a strong Republican tradition. Hughes said of his father, who had been interned in the 1940s, that "my father was a Republican, but I think, foremost, he was a socialist."[2]

Hughes, who had served in the Navy, recalled—after docking in Cape Town, South Africa, and seeing the barbarity of apartheid firsthand—that he, "was never a socialist [before, but] I certainly became a socialist during that period in South Africa [...] This had a bigger impact on my thinking as a socialist than reading books, or studying revolutionary tactics."[3]

Hughes' grandparents were also a part of the IRA, and Hughes himself continued this work by joining in 1969. Moving up the ranks in the Provisional IRA, Hughes was eventually arrested and interned in the concentration camp known as Long Kesh. Much has been written about this camp, about the

---

1   Michael Parenti, "Reflections on the Overthrow of Communism," Recorded Lecture, 1996.

2   Ed Moloney, *Voices from the Grave: Two Men's War in Ireland* (London: Hatchette UK, 2010), 41.

3   Ibid. pp. 52-53.

atrocities committed by the British; yet despite these atrocities, Hughes managed to escape Long Kesh successfully in 1973.

Hughes was eventually found by the authorities in 1974, sentenced, and transferred to the infamous H-Blocks, where he lost his political prisoner status. It was in the H-Blocks where the Blanket Protest, the Dirty Protest, and eventually the Hunger Strikes of 1980 and 1981 would take place. Hughes himself was the Officer Commanding (OC) of the H-Blocks prisoners, taking a leading role in the Dirty Protest and the 1980 Hunger Strike.

In 1986, Hughes was released from the H-Blocks—right around the time Sinn Féin began to shift their political strategy towards one which favored electoralism, in a slow abandonment of the armed struggle. As noted in several of the interviews contained in this volume, veterans of the struggle were released and forgotten, given poor jobs with poor wages. Hughes commented on his own circumstances by noting that:

> I found work on a building site on the Falls Road [in Belfast]. Some of the people I thought I was fighting for were now seeking to exploit me. I recalled my father telling me stories about earlier campaigns when Republicans such as Billy McKee came out from jail and being employed by Eastwoods for peanuts. And there I was decades later digging holes for the same peanuts.

Through political abandonment, exploitation, and Sinn Féin's movement towards reformism and cooperation with the British Government, Hughes remained committed to his revolutionary principles and steadfast to his Republican views. He continued to speak out *for* those veterans who were abandoned by the party—and he continued to speak out *against* the GFA.

Not only did Hughes fight for fellow abandoned veterans, and for the poor and working class of Ireland, but also for those affected by imperialism and colonialism world-wide— writing against the Iraq War and in support of finding justice for the Palestinians, during a time when it was taboo to do so.

Hughes sacrificed his body, mind, and his health for the Republican cause. And, even after the GFA, Hughes still continued to call for a United Ireland. Hughes was an inspiration; a revolutionary who fought until his death for working class dignity and a for a truly *free* Ireland. In murals and in spirit, Hughes' face looms large over the Lower Falls—on the International Wall, the Garden of Remembrance, and at the Hunger Strike Memorial. The people have not forgotten him.

After his death, Hughes' ashes were scattered in the Cooley Mountains of County Louth. In Irish mythology, the Cooley Mountains are where the warrior *Cú Chulainn* was slain—having tied himself to a stone so that he might die on his feet, facing his enemies. Like Cú Chulainn, Hughes died with dignity, never wavering in the face of either oppression or abandonment.

This book contains a careful selection of Hughes' writings and interviews from *after* the signing of the GFA. As such, it is a snapshot into the political climate of the North in the late 1990s and early 2000s; a snapshot of forgotten Republican veteran sentimentality and political thinking. In addition to Hughes' own words and ideas, the book also contains new essays—reflections on Hughes—from other veterans, as well as an essay from a young Republican who is a part of what many call the "GFA Generation."

Many thanks to those who graciously volunteered to contribute essays to this book, and to those at *Iskra Books* (Dave, Ben, Nate, and many more) who assisted with the editing and proofreading of this labour of love.

Go raibh míle maith agat to the Hughes family for their words, and for their donation of two letters Brendan wrote during the 1980 and 1981 Hunger Strikes. In honour of Brendan, all profits from this book will go to Ireland's homeless and hungry.

Figure 1: Company D Mural on the International Wall in West Belfast. Left to Right: Kieran Nugent, Billy McKee, Brendan Hughes.

Figure 2: Hughes' Divis Flats behind a mural welcoming people to West Belfast.

Figure 3: Garden of Rememberance in West Belfast.

Figure 4: Hughes' Memorial Bench in the Cooley Mountains.

Selected Essays from Irish Republicans

ESSAY FROM
ANTHONY MCINTYRE
April 2023

Anthony McIntyre is a former IRA prisoner who spent many years alongside Brendan Hughes in both Crumlin Road Prison and Long Kesh.

As I write on Easter Monday, a piece by a fellow *"Quiller,"* John Coulter, in today's *The Pensive Quill* reminds me that on this very day 25 years ago the final sculpting of the Belfast Agreement had just reached completion, its architecture engraved with the words Good Friday Agreement.

A Christian moveable feast day, Good Friday is promiscuous in its choice of dates, but it, rather than the 10th of April, has become the cultural site of an important anniversary. That moveability has come to symbolize the often shaky founds of the Agreement. When fuelled by goodwill, the realisation quickly dawns that within the North's political class, goodwill exists in a permanent state of drought. This has an effect similar to stock market turbulence, causing confidence to ebb as the architecture seems to sway and totter on command, usually from one side of the power-splitting ensemble within the Stormont political class.

The Agreement architecture will never actually come tumbling down. The sheer weight of the collective snouts rooting around in the trough aggregates to create a powerful anchor that holds everything in place, ensuring that all crises are temporary. Even today where there is no functioning power sharing executive to allow formal power to strut the ministerial catwalk, that situation will eventually resolve itself. The one certainty is that real power will remain where it has always been: in London.

John Coulter is a Unionist and evangelical Christian who has accompanied me on a literary journey for around two decades, frequently contributing to both *The Blanket* and *The Pensive Quill*. His father was one of the moving forces within Unionism behind the Agreement.

It might sound bizarre to the rigid binary mind that a right-wing Unionist and Christian fundamentalist would be a central figure in a blog associated with former IRA prisoners, atheists, dissenters from the GFA and socialists. One iconic Republican figure easily fitted into all four of those categories. Brendan "The Dark" Hughes had quite the radical Republican history. For many, when all is said and done more will be said than done. Brendan reversed the order of things on that front. He was a doer, a man with the ability to get things done while leading from the front.

While he never lived long enough to become a *Quiller*, he was very much a Blanket Man. Not just because he led the blanket protest from early 1978 to late 1980 before embarking on a hunger strike for political status, but because he was a key figure in the *Blanket* online journal, which flagged its ethos as a journal of protest and dissent. He was a firm advocate of free inquiry and, as part of that, he was willing from his time in prison to engage with all manner of differing opinion, including those of loyalists from the Unionist community and born-again Christians.

All of which might help explain why John Coulter is a stalwart of the current project. Like The Dark, he too on being confronted with a different idea does not collapse from anaphylaxis. He and Brendan would not have seen eye to eye on just about anything, but each had that anti-authoritarian capacity to engage with rival narratives.

This was one of the things that endeared me to Brendan from an early age. I first met him in Crumlin Road Prison in 1974, while a teenager. Although not precocious, my natural curiosity about how things worked prevented me from buying into the dominant narrative—if it failed to do what it said on the tin, I would ask "why not?" In Cage 11, Brendan—both as Cage OC and, later, as Camp OC—facilitated this culture of free inquiry. Once described by the *Sunday Times* in 1977 as having a penchant for fast cars, he had an acute reluctance to place his foot on the brake of the free-flowing of ideas, while remaining wholly bereft of the arrogance that he was somehow immune to learning from them.

Throughout his time in prison, despite being a man who was capable of commanding hierarchical military structures, he had a very egalitarian approach to learning. There was no need on his part to read Paulo Freire or to fetishize his concepts for Brendan to fully grasp the value of problem-posing learning.

At different times of the year Brendan will be remembered for different things. But in the week of the Good Friday Agreement he is remembered for his swift distillation of what the Agreement meant. It was he who coined the phrase *Got Fuck All*, a play on the GFA acronym. For someone who went under the moniker of *The Dark*, he brought remarkable light to bear on situations others tried to obfuscate.

Instinctively and intellectually, he could see beyond the guff of former comrades, some of whom tried to sell the GFA as not a transition to a united Ireland, but a transition to a transition.

Like another Republican icon, the IRA chief of staff Liam Lynch whose 100th anniversary occurs today, Brendan opted to defend the Republican project against the Treaty tradition, to which the GFA can trace its antecedents.

The Dark has bequeathed to posterity a lot of his thoughts, whether on the Irish Republican struggle, the poor, the Palestinians. Many of them came via the book *Voices From The Grave*, the interviews for which I remain honoured to have conducted.

A man with faults, foibles—and feet not grounded in clay.

ESSAY FROM
DIXIE ELLIOTT
April 2023

Dixie Elliott is a former Republican prisoner who served 9 years out of a 12 year sentence in the H-Blocks. Four and a half of those years were spent on the Blanket protest, during which time he shared a cell with Bobby Sands and Tom McElwee.

I heard the voice of Brendan Hughes a few days before I saw him in person: he was a soft-spoken man. In February of 1979 the prison authorities decided to separate the staff from the rest of the protesting prisoners in the concrete hell known as the H-Blocks—yet another attempt to break the morale of the men. I found myself being moved to H6 with my cellmate Tom McElwee, even though we didn't hold positions of leadership. I didn't get to see Brendan Hughes, known to us as "The Dark," until we went to mass in the wing canteen that first Sunday. He was huddled in conversation with Bobby Sands and other members of staff. I was seeing, for the first time, the legendary IRA volunteer we had heard so much about. He who had escaped from the Cages in the back of a bin lorry, who was a fearless freedom fighter on the streets of Belfast, and the OC of "D Company."

The Dark was small in stature with thick-matted hair and beard, his heavy eyebrows were knit together with concern and we knew that he, Bobby, and the others were talking about the men who were left to face the screws in the other blocks. The prison authorities clearly thought they could break them without the guidance of leadership, in particular the younger men in H3 where brutality was occurring on a daily basis.

The Dark, like Bobby Sands, had the well-being of the men they led at heart and we knew that this was weighing heavily on their minds. In September of that same year, we were moved back to the other protesting blocks—the isolation policy having failed due to the endurance of the men. Once again I found myself in a wing with The Dark, Bobby Sands, Tom McElwee, and others from H6. We had been put in H3 and it would be over a year before the nightmare of the hunger strikes began. I never saw The Dark again, after he had left our wing to lead the first hunger strike on 27th October 1980.

Brendan Hughes who, like Bobby Sands, had always led from the front, passed from this life on 16th February 2008 with his principles still intact. I attended his funeral with a friend, Sa Gallagher, who had also been on the Blanket protest. We looked on as those who had attempted and failed to smear his name because he refused to sell out on the ideals that so many, including the 10 hunger strikers, had died for, were jostling for position to carry or to be near his coffin.

The Dark's ashes were scattered in the Cooley Mountains above Omeath.

ESSAY FROM
JOHN NIXON
April 2023

I'll always remember my first real experience of the "Troubles" when on 14th August 1969 John Gallagher was murdered in my home town of Armagh by the notorious Tynan and Caledon B Specials—a traumatic induction to my "political" life at the age of fourteen; the beginning of a long and arduous journey that still continues over fifty years on.

So began my street political education as after this event and the massacre of fourteen innocent civil right protesters, I and many of my generation became involved in the campaign of civil and armed resistance against the oppression and brutality meted out to the nationalist people by the Unionist Orange state.

After Bloody Sunday, I joined Na Fianna Eireann at the age of sixteen and later became a member of the local republican clubs and official IRA. In April 1973, along with my comrade James "Jake" McGerrigan, I was shot and seriously wounded in Armagh city by the British army. My comrade did not survive and was buried on his eighteenth birthday.

In 1974, I was sentenced by a non-jury court to five years on weapons charges to which I strenuously pleaded not guilty. My first year in Long Kesh was a baptism by fire (literally) regarding Republican prison struggle. Horrific conditions, protests, the burning of Long Kesh in 1974, CR and CS gas, and hand-to-hand fighting on a large scale.

Later in the same year (December), many of us who had become disenchanted with the reactionary political policies and military strategy of the Officials' split from the organisation. We formed the IRSP/INLA and secured via more protests, which included a hunger strike, our own separate accomodation in Compund 14.

I was released in the summer of 1976 and on Christmas Eve of the same year, I was remanded into custody at Crumlin Road gaol. The following year I became O/C of the INLA remand prisoners and, in September 1977, was sentenced to fourteen years and embarked on the Blanket protest.

I became O/C of the INLA POWs that year and continued in this position until the hunger strike of 1980, in which I participated. The hunger strike lasted for 53 days. I was released from the blocks in January 1986, having spent extra years in prison as a result of years on the protest. Since then, I have been actively involved in community work, have worked with EXPAC (Ex-Prisoners Assistance Committee), and became involved in various local and cross-community projects promoting education, peace, and reconciliation between our communities: "Protestant, Catholic and Dissenter."

I fully support the current peace process and now believe that our ultimate objective, which from the beginning has always been the creation of a Democratic Socialist Republic, is best achieved via peaceful means.

John Nixon
Former Republican Socialist POW/Hunger Striker
April 2023

- - -

Before Brendan "Darky" Hughes came on the Blanket protest, to H-Block 5, I never met nor knew him. My first meeting with him was at mass one Sunday, the only time we had an opportunity to meet face to face—and, even then, it was for a short period as everyone had so much to contend with while maintaining important communications with others. But we still communicated while on the wings, and met again at various Sunday masses which lasted only about an hour. He was a congenial man and we got on fairly well. I was aware that he was held in the highest esteem by his comrades, by all Blanketmen, and in fact by many people inside and outside the prison, including members of the prison regime—many of whom would have known him from the Cages, and indeed by others whether they knew him or not.

I only learned about his background from other PIRA Blanketmen and, later as time passed, got to know about his deep commitment and dedication. He was a Falls Road man to the bone. The "Lower Whack" as it was referred to.

Before coming on the Blanket protest, he was a commanding officer in the compounds, but he and several others, including "Cleaky" Clarke from Ardoyne, lost their political status and were transferred to the protest blocks where he assumed command of the Provisional IRA POWs.

I had met Cleaky before when I was in Musgrave Park Hospital Military wing in April 1973 recovering from serious gunshot wounds inflicted by the British army in my native town of Armagh and while there had actually become involved in his and others' plans to escape from Musgrave at that time. But that's another story.

I recall that many lads had placed hope and expectation on the Dark's (some referred to him as "Darky") arrival to the blocks and maybe that something could or would be done to bring the never-seem-to-end protest to some form of conclusion.

It was not to be and in fact under his command the protest escalated and continued to do so until the event of the Hunger Strikes in 1980/1981. I can't recall exactly which year it was that he came onto the Blanket, maybe 1978. However, the year in which the seven of us embarked on the first Hunger Strike, 1980, was a turbulent year for our own movement, having lost our comrades Miriam Daly in June and later Ronnie Bunting and Noel Little in October.

During the Hunger Strike, I met with the Dark more often especially after the seven of us were moved to H3 where a temporary hospital wing to house us had been set up. He always made a point of keeping me up on any developments which initially were very few. But anything that gave us all hope he shared with us all during the Hunger Strike.

But even in H3 there was little opportunity for communicating with each other. Most conversations we had were either anodyne or passionate given the situation within or without the prison walls. Undoubtedly, Brendan Hughes was a deeply committed Republican socialist and that shouldn't surprise anyone who knew him or met him given his *altruistic* nature. Always thinking or caring about others and caring little for himself.

One occasion I will remember forever was the morning of Bobby Sands' death. We were in the cell together in H5. Bobby was now on his 66th day on Hunger Strike. We were all awaiting pensively for that terrible news and even when it arrived it was still a terrible shock.

The cell door opened early that morning on May 5th. The prison chaplain Fr. Toner stood in the cell doorway momentarily as though hesitating before entering. I only had to look at his visage, his eyes reddened with tears and a forlorn look about him, to immediately grasp that he didn't carry any good news. The Dark knew immediately. Fr. Toner looked at both of us and then specifically addressed the Dark. He told us that Bobby was gone. That he had passed away in the early hours. Even though the Dark expected this news it still had a devastating impact on him and indeed on us all.

Both him and Toner shed tears as the gravity of what had occurred immediately sank in. Toner still had prayer beads in his hand. The screws had allowed the cell door to be closed as they too were aware of the emotional impact of this terrible news. Both men spoke for about ten or fifteen minutes only as Toner had to return to the prison hospital where the Sands family were, as were the families of the other Hunger Strikers who were now approaching death.

To say the event was a game changer for everything and for everyone is a vast understatement. The Republican prison struggle which had slowly trundled along from March 1976 had now on May 5th, 1981, suddenly took on a whole new dimension. The Dark didn't say anything after Fr. Toner had left our cell and returned immediately to the prison hospital. He sunk deep and despondent into himself as he contemplated both the loss of his friend and comrade and as to how all this was going to pan out. I said little other than to ask now and again if he was alright or if there was anything I could do. There was usually no response. Just silence.

After short time he got up to the cell door and announced to the wing that was laden with a heavy silence that "Bobby is dead." He returned to his bed on the top bunk and lay there in total quietness. I think that morning was the lowest point in his life. I realised there was little I or anyone could do. As the day went on, he began to stir on the bed and make the odd comment regarding the fate of the other Hunger Strikers whose destiny was now in the hands of others, and I think he felt a sense of helplessness that there was little or nothing he could do.

But the Dark gradually came to terms with this history-changing event. I think that it truly challenged his enduring strength, character, and commitment. It was the only real time that I got to know the man.

We were all devasted and as the news spread throughout the protest blocks there followed in its wake a palpable silence. We could never see the fullness of the sky from within our H-Block cells, but we all sensed then that there were dark clouds on that never-seen horizon.

Everyone was lost in contemplation, in despondency, or in coming to terms with what had happened on that fateful day—and, more importantly, what was going to happen.

Brendan "The Dark" Hughes probably understood this better than any of us.

ESSAY FROM
PÁDRAIC MAC COITIR
March 2023

Pádraic Mac Coitir was born and raised in Belfast, where he has spent all of his life, apart from 15 years in prison—three of which were on the Blanket Protest.[1] Mac Coitir is a political activist involved with Lasair Dhearg. He is also a trade unionist and member of the GAA (Gaelic Athletic Association).

I was in the H-Blocks of Long Kesh with hundreds of other Republican prisoners when the IRA called its ceasefire on the 31st of August 1994. Although we weren't privy to all that was going on in the IRA, it didn't come as a surprise. We had access to newspapers and we constantly listened to the news on the radio. We also had a large number of debates on the wings and therefore we were very aware of what was going on politically on the outside.

---

1   **Editor's note**: In 1976, the British Government revoked IRA prisoners' status as political prisoners, and gave them prison uniforms to wear, instead of their civilian clothes. Kieran Nugent was the first to refuse the prison uniform, and instead wrapped a blanket around himself. He famously said, "If they want me to wear a uniform they'll have to nail it to my back."

Many of us remembered the previous IRA ceasefires of 1972 and 1975, but we believed the IRA was in a much stronger position than in those days. They were carrying out many operations in Britain and this was a big concern to the British government and capitalist elites. Sinn Féin was on the rise so overall we were confident of the position of the movement and very few of us were concerned. Of course there were cynics who warned us that the leadership may settle for a lot less than what were our publicly and privately stated objectives. Many of us were socialists and we had some concerns about more recent statements being made at public meetings about the direction in which they were going. However, we had confidence in most of that leadership, many of whom we didn't know personally.

Shortly after the ceasefire was called, IRA prisoners escaped from Whitemoor prison in England. Five were Republicans and the other was an Englishman who they trusted. Unionists and many British politicians were angry claiming this was a breach of the ceasefire, but they were ignored by the movement and their supporters.

Some of us were in contact with our female comrades in Maghaberry prison and we were discussing how the ceasefire would impact upon us. There was much speculation amongst some prisoners about the possibility of early release, but the IRA camp staff in both prisons warned against that, saying we were up against a government that had lied to us for years. One of many examples was the first hunger strike of 1980.

Talks went on between Sinn Féin and the British government, both public and private, and as time wore on it was clear there were tensions over many issues. On the 9th of February 1996, I was walking around the prison yard with two comrades when another shouted out the ceasefire had ended. We rushed into the wing canteen and watched the news on the television. Reports were coming in of a massive bomb going off in London and a big cheer went up. However, as I looked around the canteen I saw some men walk out looking despondent. They were obviously hoping the ceasefire would hold and they would be released.

Meetings were held on our wings, while the camp staff reminded the men to be cautious of reporting by the British and pro-British media, saying we would be contacted by the movement from outside. There was a lot of criticism being leveled at the IRA from the British and Free State governments as well as Unionists and constitutional nationalists. The overwhelming majority of us supported the tougher line taken by the movement.

I was released in April 1996 having served more than ten years and after settling in with my wife and two young children, I got reinvolved with the movement.

I knew a lot of women and men and would meet them on a daily basis to discuss the ongoing situation. Although I saw many positive changes, I was also concerned about how there was less emphasis on *socialism*. Some people were arguing for an end to armed struggle and to take part in constitutional politics. We all knew that more people would support Sinn Féin if the IRA ended their campaign, but many of us argued that would only be to the benefit of the British government and Unionists.

The IRA was coming under pressure from the US, the British, Unionists, the SDLP, and Free State government to call another ceasefire. Unknown to many of us, secret talks were taking place between the IRA and the above-mentioned and I would argue the pressure forced them to call another ceasefire in July 1997.

There was little, or nothing, gained for Republicans but those of us who were critical remained within the movement and tried—but failed—to influence its direction. I became more frustrated even though I wasn't arguing from a militaristic position. The goal of a Socialist Republic was no longer on the agenda, and it came down to a new neo-liberal Ireland—one that complied with a British/U.S. agenda.

The British and Free State governments knew they were winning, and they cobbled together what became known as the Good Friday Agreement (GFA). False promises were made about the people of Ireland having the final say on the outcome but it was nothing more than a sop to unionism and a jaundiced nod to "democracy." The only positive to emerge from this process was the release of Republican political prisoners. Twenty-five years on there has been little or no change, and I would argue that people have been left feeling powerless to make any meaningful change to their situation; having given their support to a revolutionary organisation that promised the Socialist Republic only to become cheerleaders for a neo-liberal project that will make no meaningful change in the day-to-day lives of the vast majority of the Irish people.

This quote from James Connolly is as relevant today as when he wrote it:

> If you remove the English Army tomorrow and hoist the green flag over Dublin Castle, unless you set about the organization of the Socialist Republic your efforts will be in vain. England will still rule you. She would rule you through her capitalists, through her landlords, through her financiers, through the whole array of commercial and individualist institutions she has planted in this country and watered with the tears of our mothers and the blood of our martyrs.[2]

---

2   **Editor's Note:** James Connolly, "Socialism and Nationalism," *Shan Van Vocht* (1897).

Selected Essays from
Brendan Hughes

LETTER TO TERRY HUGHES 1

1 November 1980

The first of two letters the Hughes family has donated to this book. In this letter, Brendan writes to his brother Terry describing the climate of the H-Blocks during the 1980 Hunger Strike.

Dear Terry,

It's been a long time since I heard from you, but your small note to me made up for that time. It really brightened up the day for me. I have been getting reports on the good work you are doing on our behalf, in fact, three days in a row from different people, so you must be getting around.

But, it is going to take an awful amount of work. The Brits are willing to kill us and, I believe, they will do it. We do have a chance to stop them, but only if we can pull the whole Irish nation behind us.

But, even if they do kill us, it must not be allowed to stop at that because they will go on doing it unless, by our deaths, the Brits can be forced from our country. This, I believe, can and must be done and you out there are the people who can do it.

Well Terry, it's not a very happy situation for any of us. I'm a bit worried about Dad. Try to comfort him as best as you can.

Give my love to Terry and family and keep up the good work. I love and miss you all very much.

Good lucky, Terry.

Your Loving Brother,

BRENDAN

1.11.80

LETTER TO TERRY HUGHES 2

5 August 1981

The second of two letters the Hughes family has donated to this book. In this letter, Brendan writes to his brother Terry, describing the climate of the H-Blocks during the 1981 Hunger Strike. As with many correspondence in the H-Blocks, this was originally written on a piece of Bible paper and smuggled out.

Well Terry I got your last letter, and was glad to hear from you. I'm sorry I have not wrote to you much. But I just can't get down to it much lately. I'm sure you understand. It's hard to believe we have eight men dead here and God only knows how many more. It got so that I'm afraid to think about it. I get lots of people telling me about the work you are doing. In fact, I got word just last night about you, and Barry from someone who does not even know you. We are all grateful to you all. Please keep it up for all our sakes.

Well young brother, it's been a long time. I think about the few nights spent with you all the time. The one thing they can not take off us in here are our dreams and memories (Thank God) and we all make full use of them. I was sort of sorry to hear you had moved out of your wee caravan. I liked that wee place. (That's because I did not have to live in it, Terry will be saying.) How is my wee sister-in-law? I'm really sorry I missed her and the kids. Let me know next time she is up. We need to have about two weeks notice before we send visits out. As you will see I'm using the good book. I hope your man does not mind. I don't believe he would. I have to go, Terry. Give my love to Jerry and the kids.

Keep up the work.

Slán,

BRENDAN

5/8/81

INTERVIEW WITH BRENDAN HUGHES

Spring 2000

Wherein Anthony McIntyre interviews Brendan Hughes, former IRA leader in Belfast and OC of Republican prisoners throughout much of the Blanket Protest in Long Kesh, for the first issue of Fourthwrite.

Anthony McIntyre: *After such long-term involvement in the Republican struggle do you feel a sense of satisfaction at the way things have turned out?*

Brendan Hughes: No. I do not feel any satisfaction whatsoever. All the questions raised in the course of this struggle have not been answered and the Republican struggle has not been concluded. We were naïve ever to have expected the Brits to get on the boat and go. But the things that we cherished such as a thirty-two county democratic socialist republic are no longer mentioned.

McIntyre: *The former Republican prisoner Tommy Gorman in the Andersonstown News bewails the absence of radical Republicanism and has questioned if it was all worth it. What is your view?*

Hughes: Let me answer it this way. When I came out from jail in 1986 having spent more than twelve years there I found work on a building site on the Falls Road. Some of the people I thought I was fighting for were now seeking to exploit me. I recalled my father telling me stories about earlier campaigns when Republicans such as Billy McKee came out from jail and being employed by Eastwoods for peanuts. And there I was decades later digging holes for the same peanuts.

McIntyre: *But there are many who feel it was worth it.*

Hughes: True. But amongst their number are those who have big houses and guaranteed incomes. Of course, it was worth it for them. I recall going to the Republican Movement and asking that it highlight the exploitative cowboy builders on the Falls Road who were squeezing the Republican poor for profit. The movement censored me and refused to allow me to speak. Once they published a piece that I wrote—or should I say did not write as the thing was so heavily censored as to be totally unrecognisable from the article I actually wrote. Some of the cowboy builders had influence with movement members. Whether true or not, there were many whispers doing the rounds that these members were taking backhanders and so on. In any event this led to a vicious circle in which money created power, which in turn created corruption and then greed for more money. Dozens of ex-prisoners are exploited by these firms. They run the black economy of West Belfast simply to make profit and not out of a sense of helping others.

McIntyre: *Is the future bleak?*

Hughes: People are demoralised and disillusioned. Many are tired but it would still be possible to pull enough together to first question what has happened and then to try to change things.

McIntyre: *But has Sinn Féin not been sucked so far into the system that any salvaging of the Republican project must now look a very daunting task?*

Hughes: While I am not pushing for any military response, our past has shown that all is never lost. In 1972 we had to break the truce in order to avoid being sucked in. In 1975 the British came at us again. And from prison through the Brownie articles written by Gerry Adams we warned the IRA that it was being sucked in. We broke the British on that but it took hard work. And now they are at it again. And it will be even harder this time. Think of all the lives that could have been saved had we accepted the 1975 truce. That alone would have justified acceptance. We fought on and for what?—what we rejected in 1975.

McIntyre: *What do you feel when you read that Michael Oatley (formerly of MI6) expresses support for the Sinn Féin leadership, and that David Goodall, who helped negotiate the Anglo-Irish Agreement in 1985 said recently that it is all going almost exactly according to plan?*

Hughes: These are the comments of men supremely confident that they have it all sewn up. What we hammered into each other time after time in jail was that a central part of Brit counter-insurgency strategy was to mold leaderships whom they could deal with. So I get so demoralised when I read about this. I look at South Africa and I look at here and I see that the only change has been in appearances. No real change has occurred. A few Republicans have slotted themselves into comfortable positions and left the rest of us behind.

McIntyre: *Has the nationalist middle class been the real beneficiary of the armed struggle?*

Hughes: Well, it has not been Republicans - apart from those Republicans eager to join that class.

McIntyre: *It seems that the social dimension is your real concern regarding Republican direction?*

Hughes: No. There is much more than that. It has been the futility of it all. From a nationalist perspective alone what we have now we could have had at any time in the last twenty-five years. But even nationalist demands don't seem to matter anymore. And in the process we have lost much of our honesty, sincerity and comradeship.

McIntyre: *But could it not be argued that this developed because people are war weary?*

Hughes: In 1969 we had a naïve enthusiasm about what we wanted. Now in 1999 we have no enthusiasm. And it is not because people are war weary—they are politics weary. The same old lies regurgitated week in week out. With the war politics had some substance. Now it has none. The political process has created a class of professional liars and unfortunately it contains many Republicans. But I still think that potential exists to bring about something different. And I speak not just about our own community but about the Loyalist community also. Ex-prisoners from both and not the politicians can effect some radical change.

McIntyre: *Do you sense any radical potential amongst Loyalist ex-prisoners?*

Hughes: Yes. Very much so. Not only are they much better than the old regime, they have experienced through their own struggle the brutality, hypocrisy and corruption of the regime against which Republicans fought for so long.

McIntyre: *What are your views on the Good Friday Agreement?*

Hughes: What is it? Have we agreed to the British staying in the six counties? If we listen to Francie Molloy that is what Republicans have signed up to. The only advantage is that unionism has changed. The landed gentry has been smashed but only because of the war, not the Good Friday Agreement. Overall, the facade has been cleaned up but the bone structure remains the same. The state we set out to smash still exists. Look at the RUC for example.

McIntyre: *Do you sense that Sinn Féin is going to settle for something like disband Ronnie Flanagan?*[1]

Hughes: Would it really surprise you?

McIntyre: *Do you sense that the Republican leadership fears or despises democratic Republicanism?*

Hughes: The response to democratic Republicanism has always been pleas to stay within the army line. Even doing this interview with you generates a reluctance within me. The Republican leadership has always exploited our loyalty.

McIntyre: *What do you say to those people who are unhappy but are pulled the other way by feelings of loyalty?*

Hughes: Examine their consciences. Take a good look at what is going on. If they agree—ok. If not then speak out.

---

1   **Editor's Note**: Ronnie Flanagan was the Chief Constable of the RUC and later the PSNI.

RADIO FREE EIREANN
INTERVIEW WITH BRENDAN HUGHES[1]

Spring 2000

John McDonagh of Radio Free Eireann interviews Brendan Hughes after the release of the first issue of FOURTHWRITE.[2]

John McDonagh: *Could you just give us your background within the Republican Movement, how you grew up, and why did you join—and how did that come about?*

Brendan Hughes: Well, I joined the Republican Movement in 1969, [...] my father had a history of Republicanism, my grandfather was in prison, my father was in prison, my mother had been arrested. I grew up in an area of Belfast which was predominantly Protestant, and growing up most of my friends were all Protestants and there wasn't a great deal of Republicanism about during my youth except through father's background. And my father would be pretty private about that, except on occasion where he would talk about his cousin being

---

1   **Editor's Note**: This is a transcript of a live interview.

2   **Editor's Note**: *Fourthwrite* was a journal produced by the Irish Republican Writers Group.

shot dead in Yard Street, and stories about my grandfather and so forth.

But in 1969 when the pogroms came about, when houses were being burnt down, when the B-Specials were shooting up Divis Street and so forth, I became involved in the movement then actively, through a cousin of mine—a guy called Charlie Hughes, who was shot dead in 1971 by the Officials, the Official IRA.

By that time in 1970, a split had occurred with the Irish Republican Army, [and] the Provisional wing of the Irish Republican Army was formed. I became involved as a member of that organization and through that—initially it was for defense against attacks by the B-Specials, the RUC, and the Loyalist mobs and defended places like Bombay Street, the areas where I lived myself, which was up the Gratton Road, [...] when the British Army came in. The war actually started then with the British Army. The British Army raided houses in the Lower Falls where I lived and looked for arms caches which the IRA had hidden, which resulted in the Lower Falls Curfew—which I was involved in. There were people there from the 40s campaign, the 50s campaign, like Bill McKee, Proinsias Mac Airt, who were long time Republicans and who had seen this as an opportunity to bring about a united Ireland. And that is actually when I got totally involved in the Republican Movement, in the Republican Struggle against the British.

McDonagh: *So were you arrested at that time?*

Hughes: I was not arrested until 1973. I had been on the run from 1970, and the British troops had raided my house looking for me, arrested my father, interrogated my father, and then released him 48 hours later to walk home with no shoes on in his bare feet. So, from 1970 until 1973, I lived in a different house every night; I moved from house to house. The British were continually raiding, to trying capture me. They actually started to—it was they who nicknamed me *The Dark*, it was they who called me *The Dark*, the British troops, but from 70 to 73 I just was constantly on the run.

McDonagh: *And how old were you at that time?*

Hughes: I was 21.

McDonagh: *And then how did your capture come about?*

Hughes: I was arrested on the Falls Road along with Gerry Adams and Tom Cahill. By that stage, the British media, the press in England, had headlined news articles about me being the commander of the IRA, or being Operations Officer of the IRA in Belfast. And we were having a meeting on the Falls Road, myself, Gerry and few others when the British Army raided the house and arrested us all. I was then taken to—we were all taken to Springfield Road RUC station where we were interrogated by ten plain-clothed British troops—British undercover operatives— and we were tortured. I was continually tortured. For over a period of up to eight hours, I was beaten with small hammers, I was tied against the wall and continually punched and kicked. I was then tied to a chair and continually beaten. They put a weapon in my—a gun, a .45—in my mouth and pulled the trigger, but obviously it didn't work. They threatened to shoot me there and dump me on the Black Mountain and put out a statement out saying that Loyalists had killed me.

McDonagh: *And what were you being charged with at that time?*

Hughes: Nothing. Nothing—I wasn't arrested with anything. I was—when they were interrogating me, they were trying to get me to sign a statement that said I was member of the IRA which I did not. So, after a period of fourteen or fifteen hours I was handcuffed, manacled, and thrown into the back of an armored car, and driven to Long Kesh where I was interned— for an indefinite period—without any charge. I wasn't charged with anything. I was just thrown into Long Kesh Internment Camp.

McDonagh: *And that how long were you interned?*

Hughes: I was there for about eight months then I escaped from Long Kesh. I escaped in a garbage truck. What happened was that I was put inside a large bag—with rubbish, sawdust, and all the garbage of the camp. The guys who came to lift the rubbish—a lorry came every day—I was thrown in the back of the garbage truck and after four or five hours in camp, the truck left, left Long Kesh and up toward the hill, I broke—I was able to release myself from the bag, jump out of the lorry, and then I had a lift actually to Newry, where I had some money coming out the jail, where I had a taxi, and I was driven to Dundalk where I was eventually free.

McDonagh: *Was there any chance of you being crushed within the garbage truck?*

Hughes: No. No, it wasn't that type of garbage truck; it was an open type truck. The danger, the biggest danger was—before the truck left the camp, a British soldier would push a large, spiked object through the rubbish—and it actually happened that day. But I had a bit of luck that day and at both times they missed, and I wasn't hit. But at that period when this happening I knew exactly what was happening, because we had done some intelligence work on it, we knew the whole process. But I took the chance. And it worked OK; they did not spike me. But I must admit at like one stage I felt like jumping up and shouting that I was here in fear of being spiked by this—it's like a large spear.

McDonagh: *And then how long were you free at this stage; how long did you stay free?*

Hughes: Well, I got across the border, I got a new identity. I had my hair dyed and changed my appearance and came back.

I was back in Belfast within ten days—1974, May 1974—I was arrested in Belfast again. I was arrested on the Malone Road, in a large house on the Malone Road, which is totally outside the working-class area. Which was a policy of mine at the time, to move outside the working-class areas, because it was becoming so hard to move around. I established an identity as traveling toy salesman and set up home outside West Belfast all together. But I was traveling into West Belfast every day with a suit and a brief case and so forth. I was often stopped by British troops and RUC, but I always got by—until the particular time when they raided the house and arrested me along with weapons and a munitions detonator and so forth.

McDonagh: *And then what were you charged and sentenced to at that stage?*

Hughes: Pardon?

McDonagh: *What were you charged and sentenced to at that stage?*

Hughes: I was charged with possession of weapons and sentenced to fifteen years—they then took me out again and charged with me escape from Long Kesh and gave me one-and-a-half years. I went into Long Kesh and—sometime in 1978 I became OC[3] of the Prisoners in Long Kesh. At one period there was a bit of riot—and, being OC, I attempted to stop the riot. But in doing that I was accused of causing the riot and I was taken out and sentenced to another five years. The morning I went to court. My position as being OC of Long Kesh, I would go out every morning and negotiate with the governor of the prison on condition and people would make requests, and I would have to sit and meet and talk to the governor and request these things the prisoners were looking for. Sometimes it was a mandolin, sometimes it was guitar, sometime it was a pair

---

3   **Editor's Note:** OC is *Oifigeach Ceannais* or Officer Commanding in the IRA structure.

of boots or medical equipment or something like that—and I would go and sit—and it would be quite cordial and quite friendly and I was called Mr. Hughes, or Host Commanding Officer. Shortly afterwards I was taken to court, sentenced another five years and I found myself put in the back of a truck and taken down to the H-Blocks of Long Kesh. I was walked in, told to strip—thrown into a cell naked—and with a blanket around me.

McDonagh: *Did they ask you to wear a prison uniform?*

Hughes: They asked me to wear a prison uniform. Yes.

McDonagh: *And then you refused?*

Hughes: I refused to wear a prison uniform yea, because I didn't see myself a criminal. I was a political prisoner.

McDonagh: *And at that stage, how long had the Blanket Protest gone on in the H-Blocks?*

Hughes: The Blanket Protest had gone on almost two years. I had been in contact with the—me being OC of the prisoners of Long Kesh, I was also the OC of the prisoners in the H-Blocks, but at no time did I visualize the conditions of the men in the H-Blocks. Until I got there. But I had put an appeal against the five-year conviction because I was—I actually had a prison officer who went and gave evidence to the fact that I was not involved in any sort of riot. I was involved in trying to keep the peace intact. But I think at that period they wanted me out of the H-Blocks and they gave me the five years. Soon afterward with the prisoners they asked me to take over, because it was totally disorganized—there was two blocks at that time there was H-5 and H-3 and there was an OC at H-5, an OC at H-3 and there was no communication at all, because at that period they were not taking visits, there was no papers, there was no radio. There was absolutely nothing at all. Everybody had long hair and long beards—I felt a responsibility to try and change that. So, I dropped the appeal against my five-year conviction and became OC of the two block H-5 and H-3. I then started to organise because I knew that the prison authorities had my people, our people, totally under control they were totally—the place was spotless clean—*screws*, the prison officers as they were called, were totally in control of this and the people there was over 150 men here at the time who were not going anywhere. So my point was we need communication. We step up the protests, we need to do something. And actually, I initially suggested—and this might be hard to believe, but it's actually true—that we put on the prison uniform—and we go into the system—and we wreck the bloody place. Just totally wreck the prison, because the way we were stuck in the cell 24 hours a day, no fresh air, no showers, no nothing. But the people that were there for two years found this very hard to take, so it was decided that we couldn't take that way. So, then I ordered that people would begin to take visits; and to take a visit, you had to put on the prison uniform. That was okay, as far as I was concerned. It was a compromise we had to make for the point of us making communication and to get more outside to what the conditions were really like. And from that we went right into the Blanket Protests and went right into the Hunger Strikes.

McDonagh: *But Brendan, before you get into the Hunger Strikes maybe you could explain how you ended up on the Dirty Protest?*

Hughes: Well, because we began to take visits, because we began to smuggle things in. We began to bring pens in, bits of paper in we began to smuggle thing out—we called them barges which is a communication wrapped up in cellifoil. It was placed up the anus, sometime up the nose, and it would be passed over sometimes in the mouth. It would be passed over on a visit. The prison authorities realized what we were doing because obviously they were raiding cells and finding pens, and finding tobacco and finding stuff. So, they introduced a mirror—a mirror search. What happened on the visit is that they came, took you out of the cell, walked you up the end corridor, and forced you squat over a mirror. We refused to squat over the mirror, so we were physically forced over the mirror so that they could look up the anus. They would then badly mistreat us—mess with us going out a visit—coming back and the shower thing. They were supposed to give a shower once a week. They wouldn't do that. Sometimes they would give—let one person go for shower, other times they wouldn't. And since most of the time when people went for a shower, they were getting physically and verbally abused. So, the order was given finally: no more showers. We stopped going to the showers. We refused to wash. So, they began to bring buckets around—buckets of water and throw them into the cell. Often just throwing them on the floor and water would spill and we supposed to wash with this. So, the order was given to smash the bases, smash the jugs. Which were plastic—we smashed all those, so they stopped doing that. It came to the point where we had to stop going out of the cells all together because of the physical abuse and verbal abuse very time we left the cell. And that's what developed into the Dirty Protest. We started to smear excreta in the cell, we wouldn't wash, we wouldn't go out and the cells just became infested with rubbish, with urine, with excreta, and the situation that they were given.

McDonagh: *And how long did that last?*

Hughes: That lasted almost three years. But it was slow development because through the protest we were making we eventually destroyed our beds, smashed them up—smashed the windows so all we were left with was a mattress, all we had was a blanket and mattress on the floor. And they would come in, most nights they would come in with hose pipes and just open the cell door and you'd get hosed down. Other times they would come in with very strong disinfectant and throw a bucket of disinfectant around you to the point where it brought tears to the eyes and was very painful. After we smashed the windows, they came I put iron grills on the windows—we were totally sealed in, and this carried on for almost three years.

McDonagh: *Was there any heat the cells? I mean was the wind coming in from these grates?*

Hughes: Yea, yea the snow, you would wake up in the morning with snow on you—yea the windows were totally open until they put the grills on. Even with the grills on, very often they turned the heat off on the cold winter nights; they turn the heat off, and, the hot summer days, they turn the heat on—they took a large machine—we used to pour out the urine out the cell doors at night and they would put this large sucker machine to let the—and leave the machine on all night. It was like a generator going all night—they left the lights on all night and as I said in the winter nights they would turn the heat off.

McDonagh: *This would bring us up to 1980; how were you able to communicate and organize a Hunger Strike within the prison?*

Hughes: We had a line of communication with the Irish language; at night we would shout the windows in Gaelic what was happening—we were able to send communications. A guy would go on a visit with a commutation—if I wanted a communication to H-Block—I was in H-Block 5, and I wanted a communication to H-Block 3; I would write a communication and give it someone going out on a visit and often other people in H-5, H-6, H-7, would meet on a visit and the communication would be passed on that way; but by and large it was done through shouting at nights the quiet nights, and Long Kesh was a very quiet place at night and we were able to shout from one block to another block, pass the communication from one wing to another wing and on to another block. That is how we done it.

McDonagh: *And how did you did come the decision about the Hunger Strike?*

Hughes: Well, because we were getting so much publicity uh because of the conditions we were in and remember that for two years these men had been sitting and no one knew anything that was going on that we were being brutalized, we were being tortured, being totally mistreated. By 1980, people were beginning to realize that there was something wrong. The main breakthrough was when Cardinal Ó Fiaich, the Catholic Archbishop—the Catholic Cardinal of Ireland—visited the prison. But he was only allowed to visit the prison or visit the people from South Armagh where the cardinal had come from, but by pure coincidence I was in a cell with a guy from Armagh and Cardinal Ó Fiaich came in and I spoke to him and he was really really touched by what he had seen and he walked out of the prison gate and he made a public statement on television that the cells looked like the streets of Calcutta—the H-Blocks.

From then on, we began negotiation with Cardinal Ó Fiaich. Cardinal Ó Fiaich began negotiations. And his contact with me was priest called Father Alec Green, and Alec was chaplain in the prison, and Alec kept contact with me and always told me that the Cardinal was doing things—the Cardinal was meeting behind the scenes—we actually began meeting another priest, Father Alec Green, he was a lovely gentleman—behind the scenes, and Cardinal Ó Fiaich went to see Maggie Thatcher, and I wasn't there at the meeting, but I was told that Maggie Thatcher was totally insulting the Cardinal. We had our hopes really built up here that we were getting a breakthrough, and I was getting word back through Father Alec Green that there are things happening—hold on, because we had been threatening Hunger Strike for about a year now and we were actual going to call one. We were all holding back, then one day I got a visit from Danny Morrison who told me—on the visit that—Maggie Thatcher had shut the door on the Cardinal and there was nothing. And we had almost four hundred men here who were sitting waiting—sitting on the blanket for years—and all their hopes were built into this—into Cardinal Ó Fiaich making some sort of progress. And here we had Maggie Thatcher just shut the door in his face. And I was told this on the visit—I got a visit from Danny Morrison, and Danny told me—he brought a cigar up for me that day, and the only the only time ya smoke was on visit. I smoked the cigar, and he told me that the door was closed, Cardinal got nothing. And I didn't know what to do. And he asked me actually, "what are you going to do now?" And I said, there was no alternative but Hunger Strike. We have to—there's nothing left except Hunger Strike. And I walked back—and it was a long walk back for the visit to the H-Blocks. I remember—I'll never forget the walk back. The prison officer beside me walking back with a long, long beard, long, long hair filthy, dirty, and walking up the path—and walking up the path into the blocks is two wings, and every face is in their window looking to see if I had any *scéal*—what we'd call *scéal* which is news—had I any news for them—and I didn't know what I was gonna tell these people—and we never ever spoke until after eight o'clock and there were only two screws left in the wing.

I was entering the cell that day and Bobby Sands was at the cell next to me. And Bobby was obviously at the pipe right away. We used to dig holes in the walls so we could communicate. And I told Bobby it's up in the air and we have to organize a Hunger Strike. Bobby absolutely was in total agreement with it and from there we started to organize the Hunger Strike. That night I got up to the door; it was half-past-eight at night when everything was quiet. None of the rest of the prisoners knew except myself and Bobby that the whole process with Cardinal Ó Fiaich had fallen through, and I then said what then happens, and that we had no alternative but to call a Hunger Strike.

And I remember the total, utter silence. That night, Bobby—Bobby had a great voice for shouting—Bobby done most of the shouting, most of the communication in the Kesh at the window—and we began the work later that night through the communications through Bobby and the Irish language. I mentioned earlier on that Long Kesh was a quiet place; it was a really silent place that night.

The next day, over the next couple of days, I got communications back in from the other block. Volunteers; I asked for volunteers for Hunger Strike. I think there was 148 volunteers—and I wanted six—one from each county. And I got 148 names in—it was only a couple of days. Myself and Bobby selected six people. Actually, Bobby wanted to go on the first Hunger Strike and I decided against it. I felt the responsibly that I should do it I called it and I should be on it. And the process started there—six of us went on Hunger Strike.

McDonagh: *You represented Antrim?*

Hughes: Yes.

McDonagh: *What was the qualification, and [was it] a tough decision to pick one from the other counties? How did they qualify?*

Hughes: It was very very hard. Very very hard to pick people. One person I had rejected was a guy called Sean McKenna—and Sean begged me and begged me to choose his name—and I eventually did. The other qualification was—there was people from the Irish National Liberation Army [INLA] there as well. And we allowed one of theirs—one from that organisation to go on the Hunger Strike. The biggest majority of the people in Long Kesh at that time were Provisional IRA people. There was a small group of INLA people, and they demanded that they had a representative on the Hunger Strike, and we agreed to that—and it was guy called Sean Nixon, a guy who was in the INLA went on Hunger Strike with us.

McDonagh: *And what happened to that first Hunger Strike in 1980?*

Hughes: The Hunger Strike went on for fifty-three days. On the forty-first day we got representation from British Civil Servants who had come in a produced this document—as an attempt to settle the Hunger Strike—we right away—at this stage six of us were within the prison hospital, and we had met in what is called the Canteen Room and we were allowed some time to discuss. We went back into our cells. Ten days later they came back again with another document which they produced, which we studied and which we believed was a possible—was possible solution to the problem.

On the fifty-third day, the day the Hunger Strike ended—a priest who was representing us met a British civil servant at a Belfast airport. And the only way that the priest could recognize this guy is that he would have a red carnation in his coat. The priest met this civil servant or whoever he was with the red carnation who passed over a document.

That night the night the hunger strike ended, Bobby Sands and the priest was in the prison hospital—at this stage—Sean McKenna was in a coma—and was almost dead. The doctor, Dr. Ross, who was our doctor at the time, told me that Sean had only a few hours to live. I believed that that we had the basis of a solution. They rushed Sean out on a stretcher.

At this stage I was still able to walk and there was two priests there, Father Murphy and Father Connor, who helped me out into the hallway when they were rushing Sean out—and Doctor Ross begged to save Sean's life. And I said it, "feed him intravenously."

Sean was—was immediately put out on support machine and the Hunger Strike was actively over. The document that the priest brought we believed was a settlement. Bobby and a priest were there with me and we believed—I couldn't read because my eyesight was gone, but the priest who had brought the document to us was overjoyed. I mean we were overjoyed as well because Sean wasn't going to die and none of us were gonna die and we had a settlement. We believed we had a settlement.

Over the next few days—I believe it was the prison regime itself that was responsible for causing the collapse of that agreement. They refused to accept clothes, they refused to accept certain pieces of clothes. Bobby had not taken over. When I went on hunger strike, I handed my position over to Bobby—Bobby Sands. When Bobby was in the negotiations, I was still recovering for the Hunger Strike in the hospital. He was in constant contact with me. They were bringing Bobby up to the hospital every day to see me.

The prison officers who were running the jail hated the whole deal. They detested us. They believed that we had won, and they done their utmost, including the Prison Governor to sabotage the whole thing. I believed they did sabotage it—and leading to the point of where Bobby sent a communication up to me that they had stopped allowing Bobby to come to see me at one stage. Bobby sent a communication to me that he didn't see any alternative here except another Hunger Strike. I fought with Bobby actually over this. I didn't believe that we should go on a second Hunger Strike. Bobby was the OC, and I was not, that's the facts as they stood, and they went on Hunger Strike. And it was Bobby's decision that the second Hunger Strikes take place.

McDonagh: *Now a significant part of this second Hunger Strike which happened in 1981 was the election of Bobby Sands to the British Parliament for Fermanagh/South Tyrone. Maybe you could describe to our audience what was that like and was that a big gamble by putting him up because had he lost it might've discredited the Hunger Strikes, but what was it like in the prison and how did you find out that we won the election?*

Hughes: Well, we—we didn't have any form of communication. Any form of communication we had we used to smuggle it in—into small pieces, small articles or whatever we had. No newspaper, no radio, no television, and when we heard that Bobby was elected, we were elated. I mean the whole world knew that he was elected before we did. We did feel that—we believed or hoped that—Jesus, this must end now, then they must give in now—they must give us our demands.

McDonagh: *But Brendan, when you were figuring out to have him run did you think it was big enough gamble that if he lost the election, it would have hurt the chances of the Hunger Strike, I mean how—what was that though process like? About that you took a gamble on it?*

Hughes: We actually on the inside didn't have a great deal of influence on that—it was the leadership on the outside that had that—and they were supremely confident, and we had a great deal of faith in the leadership on the outside, and when they decided to run Bobby in the election, we believed that it was the right decision and we believed that we should do it. And we heard the stories about the support we had out there, and we knew the sympathy was out there, so we were pretty confident that Bobby would make an impression. But we also really believed that if Bobby was elected we would—it [would] practically break the British role and we would get our demands. The thought process was dictated from the outside.

McDonagh: *And then what happen after the election?*

Hughes: Ah—Bobby died. They, they allowed him to die— and nothing changed within the prison. As I said we didn't have any sort of communications at that time at all—and all I'm doing—and all I have been doing is looking back and reading about that period, because we were totally isolated at the time a totally and totally demoralized at that time when Bobby's election didn't make any difference, and then when Bobby died—

and again the whole world knew before we knew—a priest came to my cell in the early hours of the morning after Bobby died and told me—and I knew it as soon as the priest walked into my cell—that Bobby was dead. And—it was just an abyss to us.

McDonagh: *And did you have any ceremony inside the prison?*

Hughes: Yea well, we were locked in the cell—all silence—silence—silence is—is a thing we know very well in the jail. And we had a two-minute silence thing—and that Sunday after Bobby's death that the only time we came out of our cells was—we went to mass. And we had our social mass in the jail—every wing had a special mass in the jail for that, but then the whole process starts all over again—ten died.

McDonagh: *Ah, then it was called off in the Fall and then I believe the demands were implemented by the Thatcher administration.*

Hughes: The demands were implemented, yea—the demands were implemented by the fact that that we were without—they allowed us our clothes. They gave us our clothes after the deaths—and we went out—out of our cells. And it was totally different regime all together. You know, we had shoes on, we had clothes on, we had dignity—and these same people who had tortured us all these years were still there—you went into the prison system, they forced us to work we wanted to work and sabotaged everything we could get out hands on. We broke all machines, we did everything we could do to disrupt the whole prison regime to eventually when it came to the point that they said don't—they wouldn't let us go to work anymore, so we won that demand. The demand not to work, not to take prison work. And over a period of a year all of the demands we had asked for, we had. We had our own clothes, our free association, we were treated as political prisoners, we had a representative as OC who the prison governor had to recognize. And intact we had won all the demands that we wanted.

McDonagh: *And it came at great cost.*

Hughes: It came at too big a cost I think—yes.

McDonagh: *Did it mainly have to do with Thatcher intransigence through the whole negotiation of the whole Hunger Strike?*

Hughes: Her intransigence? Yes, I think it was largely to do with that. I think that there were people there in Whitehall, in the British government who would've been quite prepared to give us what we had—what we had—I have spent almost eight years in prison with my own clothes, with political status, and here they were trying to take it away from us—and eventually they had to concede that we were political prisoners, they could not control us, they tried to control us—they couldn't we resisted every attempt to the point where ten men died—and Thatcher—Thatcher. That woman. Thatcher just could not accept the fact that we were political prisoners. We were fighting for a cause.

McDonagh: *Which brings us up to what is going on today, and I want to go back into the prison, because there's been a lot of discussion that the process that was designed in 1998 had its germs in—within the discussion group with Gerry Adams, Bobby Sands, and yourself about a way forward, a way out of what was going on. How much [were] you guys a part of that [...] process which brought us to the treaty that was signed in 1998? And was it even discussed that the way to a United Ireland was to bring back Stormont and some of the things that have come about out of the process?*

Hughes: Absolutely not. A lot of us within the prison, some of us were in our teens, some twenty-one, all young men. A lot of us went in with not a great deal of political thought in our heads. Within Long Kesh within the cages of Long Kesh, we began to push and I remember Gerry—Gerry was the main driving force behind this. That we need politically educated rank and file—politically educated rank and file—and within

Long Kesh we began to do that. We had debates, we had discussions, we had arguments, we had we had read about the Palestinian Cause, we read about the South African Cause, we debated all these causes, and we became politically educated, we became not just a soldier who was just a person who was able to fire a gun, but a person who was able to think before he fired a gun. So all that started there, I mean I was in the cages with Bobby Sands, and I was in the H-Blocks with Bobby Sands, and went through this whole situation where we became and we knew—that before we went into the prison there was Sinn Féin and there was the IRA—all the fighting we were doing, we were creating a party called—the SDLP actually became the nationalist voice of the IRA, though they were not representing the IRA but the SDLP was largely created by the war that was going on, and we knew that if you're going to fight a war, then you gotta be able to fight a war and be able to talk after the fighting stops. So, the whole sort of people who are involved in the struggle now, are politically educated ex-soldiers.

McDonagh: *Okay—now you were released in 1986 and in the interview that you did with a magazine that we will be giving out the web address[4] later on, you stated that you went to work for contractors in West Belfast and how you were reminiscing about what your father had said, that nothing much had changed after all the suffering that went on and everything that was going, that you were still be exploited by what you were calling cowboy contractors?*

Hughes: Yes. Yea. I remember the story my father used to tell me like when they all got out of jail, people like Billy McKee, me father, Proinsais Mc Airt, and so forth, they were sort of alienated by society and they could've worked anywhere, so they had to take, get any sort of work they could get. I remember—feel that—that was so sad. I mean here was people who went to

---

4   **Editor's Note**: This is the *Fourthwrite* interview that is before this interview.

war trying to bring about a Democratic Socialist Republic and they are working for these people who are exploiting [them].

When I got out of the prison in 1986, I found myself right in the same position again—I couldn't leave West Belfast, I was too well known. I couldn't have worked outside West Belfast, I had to stay here—but the only work I could get would be on a building site. And these people, they were Catholic, they called themselves nationalists, but they were doing the same and were paying people 15 to 16 pounds per day where the average would be 30 to 35 pounds per day—and that still persists today. And it's not just builders, there's loads of employers who do the same. And me being a Republican and me being involved in the Republican Struggle, one of my objectives in fighting this war and trying to bring about a Democratic Socialist Republic, was to fight for the working class. And unfortunately, I don't see that happening; I see the working class being exploited again. And being allowed—the Republicans allowing people to exploit the ordinary working man and woman, and I'm totally opposed to that.

A few years ago, I wrote an article for *An Phoblacht Republican News* against these people, and I found I had to fight with the editorial people within *An Phoblacht* to publish the thing. And when it eventually was published, it was totally censored! I wanted to expose these people years and years ago, and I wasn't allowed to. That article was printed okay, but there was no editorial, there was no campaign, there was no anything.

And all those last few years, I've kept quiet. I haven't said anything through a sense of loyalty to the Republican Movement. And do not get me wrong, I still feel and am a member of the Republican Movement, I still believe the Republican Cause, I don't believe there is anybody outside the Republican Movement that can bring about any changes. The problem, I feel, is that Republicans are sitting back and there's some of them there who have made careers out of politics and have left the principle that ten men died for, and hundreds of men died for, and hundreds of men went to jail for, have [been] left behind. And I think they need to be wakened up and it needs to be pointed out to them that, as I said in the article, it takes a great deal of pain for me to come to the point where I could put pen to paper and write this. And I do it reluctantly, but I do it through necessity and I do it through—and I also do it for my comrades who died.

McDonagh: *But Brendan, you do have people like Marian Price who have spoke out against this Agreement and then they are ostracized in Republican clubs, where she's not allowed into some. Some of the songs that were written about her in the 70s are not allowed to be sung in the clubs, I mean you're talking loyalty, but it's also a great risk within a community that you were born a raised that you're going to be ostracized for those views.*

Hughes: Yea, but unfortunately that a risk we have to take. I mean Marian and Dolours would be comrades of mine. And some of the people who would ostracize people like that, or ostracize people like me. I have no time for. Let their petty little minds ostracize right, but anyone who would want to ostracize me I would want to ask them a question: do you agree with everything the Republican movement is doing? If they do, then okay, then go away from me, I have no time for ya. If they don't agree, and they don't say anything—then I think they're a moral coward. At least Marian has the guts to stand up to and say something that she believes is wrong. I don't necessarily agree with everything Marian says, but I absolutely agree with the right for her to say, or anyone else to say what they believe in.

McDonagh: *But Brendan, one of the whole problems about this whole process is that [it] started with Gerry Adams and John Hume and it's been banged around in the press—it's called a "pan-nationalist front." Never at no time do they say it's a pan-Republican front, so it's quite obvious that Republicans had to go over to a nationalist point of view in order to join that* *front, because I can tell you in America there has always been a pan-nation-alist front with the Irish government, with Ted Kennedy, with the American Government, and with John Hume always stopping people from getting visas to come into this country so what in actual fact happened is a certain part of the Republican Movement has joined that pan-nationalist front.*

Hughes: Yes, and that's a part of it—I think that the point I'm trying to make. I think they need to be pulled back from that. I think we need to get back to the principles of Republicanism. The principles I was brought up with, the principles of James Connolly, of Liam Mellows, of true Republicanism, and I see the people—some of these people going about now—and they could just be happy to be members [of the] SDLP. And the SDLP is not a party that I would be involved with. Sinn Féin, some of the Sinn Féin Leadership now, I don't want to be involved with them. I want Republicanism back to its roots.

McDonagh: *But then they'll tell you then the doors will shut, the visas will stop, we'll not get into the White House on St. Patrick's Day, the fundraising will stop in America, and we'll be an isolated party. Whereby if we have all these doors open maybe we can make some progress, but there is a price to open those doors.*

Hughes: Well, I mean, if you have all the doors open and you walk through the doors and leave yer children behind, what the hell is the sense of leaving the doors open if you leave your children behind?

We're talking about the Republican family here, a family that's been fighting a war for so many years, I think if you are honest and sincere and you stick by the ideas that you fought for, then so what if the doors close, then kick them down some way. I mean there no use have these doors open if actually you're leaving everything behind now. And I'm afraid that there are some people in the leadership who are prepared to do that.

I talk to people every day on the ground, and most of them

ex-prisoners, and all Republicans, and most of them are very unhappy with the way things are going, and I know the point that your making—you have to get some doors open somewhere—but I don't think you should have to leave your principles behind to do that.

McDonagh: *You're Listening to Radio Free Eireann, and this will be aired on St. Patrick's Day. We're speaking with Brendan Hughes, who is the former OC of the H-Blocks and in Long Kesh, and we started off with his background being in prison and now we're going to what we find in 1998. Now Brendan, in your wildest dreams, when you were fighting to bring down the local government in the six counties called Stormont, did you think that you would see a day where you actually have Sinn Féin begging the Loyalists to go into Stormont and actually having administering British rule in Ireland and being paid by the British to do it? Now in your article you stated you think there was an insurgency program going on by the British government to mold a Republican leadership that they can deal with. Maybe you can explain how this came about where you now have member of Sinn Féin fighting to get into a British government in the six counties?*

Hughes: Yea—it something I could never visualize my wildest dreams, I never visualized that whatsoever. The problem is like in 1972 the ceasefire—the IRA cease-fire the British Government tried to get people involved in this long-drawn-out ceasefire just to end the war and it was recognised within a period of two weeks—it was recognized, and the war was back on again.

In 1975, they released certain people, they arrested certain people and released certain people. Gerry Adams was one of the people arrested I was one of the people arrested. They released other people from the prison who became the leadership in the Republican movement. And within the prison, people like myself and Gerry opposed the ceasefire, and some of the articles Gerry wrote many articles warning the leadership that you're getting drawn into long drawn-out ceasefire, the British are trying to stop the war. And their trying to mold the type of people they can deal with. And as I said they selectively released people from prison knowing they would be in the leadership and knowing their profiles and knowing the British could deal with them.

In the 90s, I think they have done the same. They have allowed a leadership to develop. They have pumped millions into here. I mean there's centers all over the place in West Belfast and North Belfast, people have gone into these centers and become career people and they are being paid very decent wages, certainly a lot more than the people in the building situation were being paid, and the British have encouraged this—and here ya have other people—to the point where ya have people breaking away forming the Continuity IRA, the Real IRA—which I am not a supporter of, I think the leadership needs to look at itself and needs to find out, are they playing the Brits' game here? And I believe they are. I mean going into Stormont, the contradiction of a Republican begging Loyalists to go into Stormont. It's just so hard for me to swallow.

McDonagh: *Also we had Martin McGuiness stating in this country that when these vote were taken, that he was voted in by the Irish people and he was voted by the Irish people to administer British rule in Ireland, but then the rug was pulled out from under him when they just passed a law in London negating any vote that just took place in Ireland and just made unless you play the game, we can give you your role to be a Minister and we can also take that away.*

Hughes: That—that's exactly what I think: the whole thing's been just a farce. It never ceases to amaze me how we have allowed ourselves to get into this position where the British control everything here, they still control everything here the RUC's still here, the whole structure's still here the judiciary is still here, the murder machine's still here, and I mean hospitals are getting pulled down, schools are getting funds cut. We find ourselves in a position where Republicans are administering this, and we don't have any control.

How far down the line do we go here? Do we start putting on wigs and joining the judiciary, the British judiciary, and start administering British justice in Ireland? At the moment or when the assembly was going, we were administering British rule.

How far—how far do we go here? To me, the whole thing seems to me sometimes to be a complete farce. I mean, where the hell is Republicanism going? All I'm trying to do—I don't have an alternative; people keep saying to me if you're going to criticize, put up an alternative. I don't have an alternative; the alternative is within the Republican movement. I think there has to be an open an honest debate.

You heard about the Hume/Adams Document—what is it? Have you seen it?

McDonagh: *Nope.*

Hughes: I haven't seen it. I don't know what it's all about! What was said or even came out of the document that brought this whole process about? I don't know.

The reason why people like me and Anthony McIntyre and the rest of the people that are involved with the writers' group, we want to know what's going on? And we don't know what's going on, we can see what going on but what's the purpose anymore?

McDonagh: *But a lot of it, Brendan, and you can see a lot of people just walking away from the movement saying, "listen I've given so much of my life I can't do it anymore," and take some of the benefits which are coming in, some of the economic benefits that are coming and people are getting disillusioned. I mean how are Republicans to overcome that when there are job opportunities opening up and if you take the road you're taking those job* *opportunities are going to get very small?*

Hughes: We're not talking about job opportunities here. There are people in jobs. Okay, I mean I'm not in a job, thousands of people aren't in a job—there's 1,800 people who lost their jobs this morning cause people just closed down the shipyard. What are we talking about here? I'm talking about the *Republican Cause*, I'm talking about justice, about working for people's right for a job; I'm not talking about a handful of selected people walking into well-paid jobs and having good salaries. And even that with all these people I'm talking about within well-paid jobs, it can stop tomorrow if the British decide to pull the plug. These well-paid jobs and these people who are in jobs have no control over their own lives!

There's 1,800 men who lost it in the shipyard today. I mean, I don't want that. They have no control over that. So, I mean we're talking about jobs here, I mean you can have a job, but have no security. I want a job and I want security in that job, and I want a job for my son and a job for my daughter, I want security! I want to have control over that. A job's a job but security, is the most important thing.

McDonagh: *Well Brendan, we've been almost speaking an hour here and I am very grateful for putting on the record for how we've gotten to the point where we have gotten to. What do recommend we do particularly in here in America and we have a lot [of] Republican people living in the tri-state area and people will be listening on the internet, who were forced to come to this country because some of the things that are going on.*

Hughes: I think they should look at the situation, look at the background, look at the history of what Ireland has done to itself. Look at the people in America you're talking about now, who had to leave Ireland. I don't want to have to leave Ireland, I don't want my children to have to leave Ireland, what I think we should do is talk, debate, if you think there is something wrong, say it! It may hurt some people, but if you believe you're right, I think you should speak up. I think people should have a great look and not be carried away by the mass media stuff— look into the belly of the beast and see what's really happening, and—I know so many people here in Belfast and throughout Ireland who are disillusioned and who are walking away and who just don't see any hope, but what I would hope to be able to do, would be to give them a view where they can feel able to contribute to the debate. And I think the debate is the most important thing and it's their way out of this and [to] look back into Republicanism and what is Republicanism all about? And that is all I would want them to do.

McDonagh: *Yea, Brendan, in this country too, people in Irish Northern Aid and the Clan na Gael are always being marginalized. There is this looking up there, saying look we're in the White House, look there's a picture of Gerry Adams dealing with Clinton, and I would have to believe a lot of people on the Falls Road would say look how far we've come look at the pictures. We're on the front page of the New York Times, there's been clubs or business that you couldn't get involved with and now allowing in people with Republican backgrounds to get involved with and people are looking at this as a way forward, that this as it's a great thing that's happened.*

Hughes: I would say—I have a house, and I paint the whole outside of it beautiful, and inside the house there's no furniture. What the hell use is the house?

DOES ANYONE CARE?

Autumn 2000

Fourthwrite *No. 3*

Does anyone care? That was a question so often shouted in desperation by cold, hungry, naked men behind closed doors in the H-Blocks of Long Kesh. Silence can often be a comforting, peaceful and reflective period, but the silence of the H-Blocks was a deadly frightening experience often shattered by the sound of baton wielding, sectarian screws bursting into some kid's cell, leaving him battered and bloodied. The occupying forces had taken their revenge on one more dissident Republican who dared defy and disagree with the rules and regulations laid down by the British Government.

An Irish Republican is a dissident first and foremost. It is dissent from British occupation that leads the Republican to the battlefield, jail, or the cemetery. Part of the Republican's struggle is against a strategy of labelling which depicts Republicans as something other than the norm—the British did it as far back as the Punch cartoons of the ape-like Irish figure. In the seventies we were called Godfathers, gangsters, Al Capones and criminals. Unfortunately, the British have had no monopoly on labelling. In 1975, myself and other Republicans in the cages of the Long Kesh were labelled by the IRA's jail leadership as "pro-British elements" and "anti-IRA" for questioning the strategy of the then "Republican leadership."

Again today, some Republicans have eagerly jumped on the bandwagon and are now labelling fellow Republicans who dissent from the present political process. The only way to avoid being labelled a dissident it seems is to accept the status quo—but then that would leave us in a position of no longer being Republicans. Just what the British would love.

For years, indeed generations, Republicans have had to fight for everything won within the prisons. Many Republicans, against the advice of the leadership, disagreed with some of the tactics used to try and secure our demands during the blanket protest. Some Republican prisoners dissented by refusing to come out of their cells at any time even to go on visits or attend Mass even though the vast majority of prisoners did so. Others dissented by refusing to go on the blanket because they believed it to be degrading to the cause. That was their right. It is quite legitimate for a Republican to dissent from the leadership. Now some dissident Republicans find themselves back in prison. And again they are being labelled and criminalized. People like myself need not support the activities of those now in prison but we must acknowledge that they are political prisoners. Are we to prompt those prisoners to ask as we did: "does anyone care?"

SO WHY DID WE STRIKE?

8 October 2000

What are we doing in Stormont going through this degrading charade? Have we accepted that because we may have lost the military war, we must also humiliate ourselves and abandon the political war? Have we accepted that Stormont is now okay; that the RUC is no longer rotten if Patten is implemented? Have we accepted that we are really British after all? Is it not more true to say that we have deluded ourselves and our own people by pretending that we have won a better deal for the working people of Ireland? As a fellow blanket protester has said—all of this is the British government's alternative to Republicanism. What are we doing accepting it?

I am not advocating dumb militarism or a return to war. Never in the history of Republicanism was so much sacrificed and so little gained; too many left dead and too few achievements. Let us think most strongly before going down that road again. I am simply questioning the wisdom of administering British rule in this part of Ireland. I am asking what happened to the struggle in all Ireland—what happened to the idea of a thirty-two county socialist republic. That, after all, is what it was all about. Not about participating in a northern administration that closes hospitals and attacks the teachers' unions. I am asking why we are not fighting for and defending the rights of ordinary working people, for better wages and working conditions. Does thirty years of struggle boil down to a big room at Stormont, ministerial cars, dark suits and the implementation of the British Patten Report?

What has been shown here is that no matter what Nationalist politicians say about all of this they merely spend what the British allow them. Their grasp on political power is no stronger than my grasp on special category status. One morning in January 1978 I was the "officer in charge of the Republican prisoners" in Long Kesh; in the afternoon I was "704 Hughes" by edict of the British government. In the morning I was a political prisoner—in the afternoon the British deemed me a criminal and left me naked in the H-Blocks. The nationalists' power at Stormont, like my clothes, the British consider to be a privilege—something to be taken away at any time. All Republicans have gained are smoke and mirrors and nothing of substance. The British control the show and are always willing to follow the logic of the Unionists.

It seems now that we have even reached the stage, as in Animal Farm, where some Republicans are more equal than others. If the reports from Stormont are correct then it would seem that a senior member of Sinn Féin—who would proclaim himself quite green—has discriminated against other Republicans on the false tactical grounds that they "are too identifiably Republican" to be employed in the Sinn Féin ministries.

For thirty years we sought to destroy this bastion of hatred and bigotry. Throughout its history the British fed it and bred it. Are we really expected to believe that the British alternative to Republicanism—the Good Friday Agreement—will see Britain destroy its own baby? I don't think so.

If, as some tell us, a united, just and egalitarian Ireland is so close why are there still Republicans taking up arms and risking their lives in order to achieve it? Are we going to be part of an administration that tortures and interns them? Where will it end? Twenty years ago, this month a hunger strike began in the H-Blocks of Long Kesh. Twenty years on there are Republicans in prison such as Tommy Crossan. British troops are still on the streets; the RUC are still there, whether Royal Ulster Constabulary or Patten Ulster Constabulary.

Our experience up to now has been humiliating. We have danced to every tune; broke every promise ever made; pursued all the policies we used to term others "collaborators" for pursuing; and have dressed it all up as something progressive in order to deceive our base. Have we merely proved the old adage that the first casualty of war is the truth?

I understand that articles like this written by people like me cause annoyance to some fellow Republicans. That is unfortunate but so be it. It is my very Republicanism that causes me to speak out just as it did during those long and lonely years on protest. My Republicanism then was legitimate—it is no less legitimate today. Twenty years ago they called me a Fenian bastard. I remain an unrepentant Fenian bastard. My Republicanism and hunger strike were against British rule. I still refuse to conform to it or the views of those now administering it.

DANCES WITH BUFFALOS

Winter 2000/2001

FOURTHWRITE *No. 4*

The race to catch up with the great capitalist buffalo, that same great capitalist buffalo that feeds us, clothes us and makes us rich—but not all of us; in fact only a few of us—is infectious. Along the trail to catch the great buffalo we see the hoof prints of those who went before us. Oh the lucky ones they are. They sit smoking their pipes, drinking their brandy. Indifference makes the race go on—never mind the starving spectators, just don't take your eyes off the prize. Keep your eyes on the pipe and brady. Keep your eye on the buffalo. Just make sure you get into the dance hall of the rich.

After all, haven't they all done it? Russia, the great bear, for so long the dream of non-buffalo chasers. Enlightened Europe, for so long the intellect of the world, now with its millions of poverty-stricken children. Ireland, a bastion of resistance to those trampled in the path of the buffalo, has caught its own and now chases the tiger.

The problem with chasing the buffalo is that like Lot's wife, you cannot look back on the trail—you must never look back.

To do so will show the price that others must pay for you catching the buffalo. The price in terms of human suffering that has paid for the brandy, pipe and log cabin is a costly one. For the trail is littered not with the corpses of buffalos but with human bodies, blood, sweat and tears. And still those millions live in poverty in Europe alone. Don't look back or you will lose sight of the buffalo, lose sight of the pipe, brandy and log cabin in which you reside warm and comfortable while the poor scrimp and save, out of your vision. Tommy Gorman is right. He forces us non-buffalo chasers to ask has the working class been left behind? So what is the answer? For humanity's sake look back. Come out of your second homes in the country and come back to the people whose blood built them.

INTERVIEW WITH BRENDAN (DARKIE) HUGHES

24 November 2000

First published in the San Francisco-based monthly newspaper, THE IRISH HERALD.

INTERVIEW WITH JOE O'NEILL

In last month's *Irish Herald,* we ran a short piece on "The Irish Republican Writers Group." In this issue, a founding member of the group, Brendan (Darkie) Hughes, airs his views on his Republican philosophy and questions the political direction of the current leadership of Sinn Féin and the Republican movement.

Hughes was one of a small group of Republicans in the Lower Falls (Belfast), who split from the IRA in 1970, to form what was later to be known as the Provisional IRA. In the sometimes violent split within the movement at that time one of the first victims was his cousin, Charlie Hughes, who was shot dead in a gun battle in the Lower Falls by members of the Official IRA.

After almost three years on the run, Hughes was arrested,

along with Gerry Adams. They were tortured for over 12 hours in Springfield Road barracks and then Castlereagh before being flown to the cages of Long Kesh. Within 5 months Hughes had escaped from Long Kesh, crossed the border and within 10 days, was back in Belfast with a new identity, to assume command of the Belfast Brigade.

Captured again 6 months later, he was sentenced to 15 years on weapons, explosives, and documents charges. Hughes, as Brigade OC was caught with what the press called a "Doomsday Plan" which was the IRA plan for the defense of the Nationalist community in Belfast.

While OC Republican prisoners in Long Kesh Hughes was charged in connection with a prison riot and given an additional 5 years. However, at this time, the process of Ulsterization and criminalization had begun and he was taken from court to the infamous H-Blocks. "That morning," said Hughes, "I left Long Kesh, Brendan Hughes, OC Republican prisoners, recognized as a political prisoner and that afternoon, I was Hughes, 704, in the H-Blocks."

In the H-Blocks Hughes was instrumental in organizing the men on the blanket protest and was elected OC with Bobby Sands as his adjutant. As the protests by the men escalated, without any movement by prison authorities, or the Thatcher government, to resolve the prisoners demands to end their inhumane treatment, he called for volunteers to join him in a hunger strike. Hughes resigned as OC, to be replaced by Bobby Sands and was joined by 6 of the 90 men who had volunteered to go on hunger strike. After 53 days without food, with Sean McKenna within hours of death and the others in very serious condition, the strike was called off as the government delivered a document which satisfied the prisoners demands. After the government reneged on their agreement the strike led this time by Bobby Sands commenced with deadly consequences.

In an interview with the *Irish Herald*, Hughes discussed a wide range of topics on the Irish political landscape.

THE GOOD FRIDAY AGREEMENT

"The decision was taken from the top down, there were no discussions, there was nothing taking place. What we heard was, 'The Hume/Adams Document' and I am very annoyed at this because, I have spent my whole life in this Republican movement and all of a sudden everyone is talking about 'The Hume/Adams Document' and I asked if I could see it. To my knowledge no one has ever seen it. I thought it was a disgrace that John Hume knew where this movement was going, but I didn't know where it was going. I didn't know anything about 'The Hume/Adams Document', what the hell is it? Then, 'The Hume/Adams Document', developed into the 'Good Friday Agreement'. What was the Good Friday Agreement all about? All of my life I spent attempting to bring down Stormont, attempting to remove the British from Ireland and all of a sudden, all of that language was gone. We no longer talk about a British declaration of intent to withdraw from this country and we have got to the stage where we were actually fighting to get down to the Stormont, that we just spent 30 years trying to bring down. The loyalty factor eventually burnt out with me, the loyalty factor was no longer there."

SINN FÉIN LEADERSHIP

"Stormont is OK as long as we're in it. What was developing here was a sort of a class thing within the Republican movement. You had the 'Armani Suit Brigade' and a lot of these people I had never come across before. I had never spent time in prison with them and their politics drifted away from me, their politics, I didn't drift away from my politics, their politics drifted away from me to a stage where I believed I needed to say something, because these people are running away with my movement. The suffering and everything that we represented was no longer there anymore and these people had it, they were wineing and dining at Stormont. I believe very shortly, we will be wineing and dining in Westminster. I believe that they have run away with the politics, the real politics of the Republican movement the Republican struggle and I believe that they have to be resisted. Which I am doing. It wasn't easy for me to go public and criticize all these things that were going on, but I feel a moral responsibility to do so. Even though it puts me on the fringe and I am called a dissident and other names. But I know damn well, that what I am saying is representative of the ordinary people on the ground."

THE REPUBLICAN MOVEMENT

"I believe this Republican movement belongs to the people. I don't believe that people like me should walk away and form another small group to oppose this group. This group is the Republican movement. We have fought, we have gone through an awful lot of struggle and I believe it has been hijacked by a handful of people who have gone in a particular direction that I disagree with. But it is my movement. I don't want to form another movement, I want my movement back to what we fought for. I don't believe that it is totally hopeless. I believe it can be won back. If I thought it was hopeless, I would probably leave the country. I believe that I have a moral responsibility and a duty to carry on the struggle. It's not easy, a lot of the people I am talking about are comrades and friends of mine. I wish they could change and turn this thing around and bring it back to the people. Bring the movement back to the people. Not a political party that's running to Stormont, running to Westminster with their Armani suits on and jutting about in their State cars. The same regime that's been oppressing us for so many years, they have become a part of."

DECOMMISSIONING

"The IRA has been asked to decommission. We were all told that there would be no decommissioning. When you bring a stranger to a dump, an IRA dump, and point out where that dump is to me that is decommissioning. I certainly would not go near that dump again, so that dump is, by and large, decommissioned. Forget about it. It has been identified yet I am told there will be no decommissioning. To me that is decommissioning. People are telling lies. We are doing everything we were told would not happen. We still hear at some commemorations people getting up on platforms and telling blatant lies. 'The war is not over'. By and large, the war is over. The current joke in the town at the moment is; 'Q. 'What is the difference between a Sticky (Official IRA) and a Provie (Provisional IRA). A. Twenty years.' The only difference is that the Stickies didn't have to decommission."

THE RUC

"What I was beginning to see was the reintroduction of a different type of philosophy, the words they were using 'the RUC has to be changed' no longer disbanded."

COMMEMORATING THE 20TH ANNIVERSARY OF THE HUNGER STRIKE

"Anyone who is going out to commemorate the Republican struggle should commemorate the people who died in the struggle. It should be about respect and to commemorate the sacrifice that these people made. I believe the party of the working class is entitled to commemorate the working-class people who died. I believe a party of the middle or upper-class should not be allowed to capitalize on those people's deaths. Those people died for working-class issues and I believe that the only people who should be allowed to capitalize on that are working-class people who are fighting for working-class issues. I don't believe the leadership of the Republican movement, at present, is fighting for working-class issues, or fighting for the issues that these people died for."

ARMED STRUGGLE

"We are sitting in Divis Towers now and there is $10 million of equipment on top of this roof, there are armed British troops on top of this roof. As long as there is one British soldier on this roof, I believe that people have a right to oppose that. Unfortunately, the occupation forces are still here and unfortunately, the leadership of the movement that I belonged to have become a part of that, they have become a part of the problem."

IRELAND:
"A BETRAYAL OF WHAT WE FOUGHT FOR"

2000 December

Fight Racism, Fight Imperialism *Interviews Brendan Hughes*

At the beginning of December 2000, Brendan Hughes, along with Antho-
ny McIntyre, spoke at a meeting in Manchester on the situation in Ireland.
At it they both outlined their opposition to the Good Friday Agreement and
the role that Sinn Féin is playing. They both belong to the Irish Republican
Writers Group (IRWG) which produces the magazine Fourthwrite. Both men
were IRA POWs held in Long Kesh. Brendan Hughes was the Commanding
Officer of the prisoners when the first hunger strike began in 1980 and he was
himself one of the hunger strikers. After the meeting, Brendan kindly agreed to
be interviewed, first telling how he had been held and questioned for 1 1/2 hours
at Liverpool Docks before being allowed entry to Britain.

Fight Racism, Fight Imperialism: *What are your views on the*
peace process?

Brendan Hughes: I basically strongly agree that the war
in Ireland with the British is over. I believe that the military
struggle is over but I totally disagree with the Good Friday
Agreement (GFA). The Republican Movement, the IRA, spent

30 years bringing down the rotten regime called Stormont, controlled by the British government. The GFA has brought Sinn Féin into Stormont, still controlled by the British, with the RUC still armed and still on the streets. British troops are still on the streets of the north of Ireland, still on the roofs of the Divis Flats. Sinn Féin people have now become part of the occupation forces in the north of Ireland. I disagree with that. I disagree with the whole concept of administering British rule in Ireland, which I believe Sinn Féin is now doing. I therefore will oppose it.

The GFA allowed two Sinn Féin ministers into Stormont. One of the acts the Sinn Féin Health Minister carried out was to close a hospital. [Bairbre de Brun, Sinn Féin Health Minister, carried through cuts in the health budget. Hospital facilities in South Tyrone and the Jubilee in Belfast have been closed. She is also introducing the Private Finance Initiative into the Royal Victoria Hospital in Belfast.] I believe that as long as Sinn Féin are in this regime, then they are in a British regime and they are administering British rule in Ireland. I totally disagree with what's happening and I'm opposing it, but it's not easy. I've been a member of this movement for over 30 years, most of my adult life. It doesn't make it easy. I don't feel comfortable about it, but I know it's right to oppose it because what's happening is, I think, a total betrayal of everything the Republican Movement has represented over the years.

I think the Republican leadership has begun to move away from everything that we fought for and I'm saddened over that. Again I have to say, it's not an easy thing for me to do. They are my old friends and comrades, but for me it's wrong, very much wrong and I have to speak about it.

FRFI: *Why do you think this process is happening? Whom does Sinn Féin represent?*

Hughes: I think Sinn Féin is changing. I've noticed it over the years. I've written to *An Phoblacht*, the newspaper of Sinn Féin, and tried to expose the rogue builders on the Falls Road —rogue builders that are paying men £20 for a day's work, way under the rate. That was my first act, to go and write an article and try to get it published in *An Phoblacht*. When they read the article at the *An Phoblacht* office, they refused to publish it. I threatened the editor that if they didn't publish it, I would go to the Irish News with a stronger version. The article was eventually published, very much watered down. To the present day those same rogue builders are still there paying the same wages with the complicity of the Sinn Féin leadership. To me it's a betrayal of the working class. To me it's a shame, a disgrace that they are allowed to get away with this and these same builders that I've been writing about, campaigning about, are building Sinn Féin offices! They're still paying the same wages. They pay their men in pubs, they allow the men to run up bills, to me they're just alien to everything Republican, everything revolutionary that I've ever stood for in my life. It shouldn't be allowed to happen.

A new type of leadership has come in who are "collar and tie"—all the woolly jumpers have been thrown away and the collars and ties are in. From my perception of things the Republican leadership has moved away from the working class and is attempting to win the middle class. They're attempting to win the ground that belonged to the SDLP.

FRFI: *Do you see any way forward?*

Hughes: I don't have an immediate alternative. The only alternative we're expressing through the IRWG is debate. I think debate has been muffled and censored. I think debate has been unwelcome. I think the way forward for us at present in the IRWG is to try and expose the weaknesses and the betrayal of the GFA and to force people to answer the questions that we have asked. To build a broad base of debate initially, to try and force the Republican Movement back to the base where it belongs, in other words the working class. As to building another party, I am certainly not attempting to do that. I think the people who can bring about a revolutionary socialist party in Ireland are in Sinn Féin. If the little that we are attempting to do in the IRWG goes any way towards that, then OK, that's an achievement on its own. If all that fails, at least what we're trying to do is record that not everyone could go along with Sinn Féin's acceptance of the GFA and the British solution to the Irish problem. At least we'll be on record of trying to oppose it and of sticking our necks out. If we achieve more than that, then great, we can develop from there.

Everybody is opposed to the IRWG—the British, the British media, the Irish media, the Republican media, everyone is opposed to what we're trying to say. To me that says we must be doing something right.

Brendan Hughes was the Commanding Officer of Republican POWs in the H-Blocks in 1980 when the first hunger strike began and was one of the first seven hunger strikers. The hunger strike was the culmination of the struggle of the prisoners for the right to be classed as political prisoners, a right taken away from them by the Labour government in 1976. The hunger strike began on 27 October and on 1 December three women prisoners from Armagh joined the protest. Mass demonstrations took place throughout Ireland and across the world. On 15 December, another 23 prisoners joined the hunger strike, followed the next day by a further seven. The health of Sean McKenna, one of the original hunger strikers, was at this point severely deteriorating. British Secretary of State for Northern Ireland Humphrey Atkins issued a document to the hunger strikers indicating that their demands would be met. The hunger strike was called off. The British government reneged on the deal and a second hunger strike began, leading to the death of ten hunger strikers.[1]

1   **Editor's Note:** The preceding paragraph is Hughes' short bio from the original FRFI Interview; republished in *The Blanket.*

HUGHES NO LONGER TOES
THE PROVO LINE

17 December 2000

SUNDAY TRIBUNE

Brendan Hughes expresses his anger towards one-time brother-in-arms, Gerry Adams, and others in the "Armani Suit Brigade."

ARTICLE BY NIALL STANAGE

Brendan Hughes looked out onto the Falls Road. A man sitting in a car opposite the safe house had aroused his suspicions. Hughes asked someone from the area to check him out. When the local approached, the man drove hurriedly off.

Moments later, British troops swarmed through the door, pumped up with adrenaline, shouting, jostling. They were soon exultant. They had captured not just Hughes but two of his senior colleagues in the Belfast IRA. One was Tom Cahill, the other Gerry Adams. It was 1973.

A lot of blood has been spilt since then. The lives of Adams and Hughes have diverged to an even-greater extent, too. For the former, the tortuous grind of the peace process has been enlivened by electoral triumph, White House welcomes, the international respect accorded to a burgeoning statesman.

Brendan Hughes gets by on income support. His last job was as a hod-carrier on a building site. We meet in a flat in Divis Tower. The top floor and roof of the complex are home to the British Army—its observation post has been there for years and, for all the talk of demilitarisation, the army shows no inclination to abandon it.

Hughes is angry. He believes that the Republican movement to which he has devoted his life has drifted from its base, betraying its principles and its working-class roots. He referred to those in control as "the Armani Suit Brigade."

Hughes has only recently begun to voice these criticisms openly in the recent past. "There's an old cliché in the Republican movement: 'stay within the army line.' That's what I did, but I was making no progress whatsoever," he said.

Even so, his first public pronouncements were circumspect. Now that has changed. The final straw came when Real IRA man Joseph O'Connor was shot dead in Ballymurphy in October.

"When people get into positions of power, and start enjoying the trappings of power, people like Joe O'Connor get killed in the streets," Hughes commented bluntly.

No paramilitary group has accepted responsibility for the killing, and the security forces have declined to say who they think is to blame. Such a convenient silence doesn't wash with Hughes.

"If that's right, then let's have a bloody inquiry, because it means there's a bunch of men running around Ballymurphy killing people and nobody knows who they are."

So Hughes thinks the Provisional IRA killed O'Connor? "I

do, yes. I feel disgusted, I feel hurt, and I feel it's a total contradiction of everything Sinn Féin are saying. Everybody knows who done it."

Hughes went to O'Connor's funeral and helped carry his coffin. In the clannish world of Belfast Republicanism, it was seen as an important gesture, though Hughes pointed out that he was expressing his opposition to O'Connor being killed, not support for the Real IRA.

"Why didn't Gerry Adams go to his funeral?" he asked. "He was one of his constituents. Joseph O'Connor was a Republican who was shot."

As allegation and counter-allegation flew in the wake of the killing, mainstream Republicans mounted pickets on the homes of Anthony McIntyre and Tommy Gorman, two non-aligned dissenters. Hughes was not impressed.

"Anthony McIntyre and Tommy Gorman came out with a totally honest appraisal of the situation and they were picketed. I see paranoia [within] the leadership; anybody who criticises must be condemned, there must be no debate, 'we must not be questioned'. We have something that is almost fascism developing out of this, and that is scary."

Disturbed by the anger he had seen among young Real IRA supporters at O'Connor's funeral, Hughes also realised that a full-blown feud between RIRA and the Provisionals was a possibility. He and veteran Republican Billy McKee offered their services as intermediaries.

Word soon came back from the Provos that Hughes was "not acceptable." It was the most pointed of snubs.

"I have spent 30 years of my life in this struggle," he said. "I know what I wanted 30 years ago, and I don't see anything close to it at the moment. I just see the movement which I spent my life in becoming part of the corrupt, rotten regime which we tried to destroy."

Does he feel betrayed?

"I do, yes."

Anyone close to the current leadership seeking to disparage Brendan Hughes will not have an easy task. Very few members of the IRA have such a dramatic record of activism as the man known as 'The Dark.'

Hughes was approached to join 'the movement' in 1969. He made swift progress through the ranks and was soon one of the senior IRA men in his area. Asked if he was Belfast commander of the IRA, he replied, "So they say," and smiled.

He went on the run in the city in 1970. It was a chaotic time. "On a normal day in the '71-'72 period, you would have had a call house [a safe meeting place] and you might have robbed a bank in the morning, done a float [gone out in a car looking for British soldier] in the afternoon, stuck a bomb and a booby trap out after that, and then maybe had a gun battle or two later that night."

During the same period, Hughes survived an attempt on his life by British soldiers. He still bears a bullet scar on his forearm.

When Hughes arrived in Long Kesh in 1973, after his arrest with Cahill and Adams, he thought his war was over. Instead, he soon escaped, rolled up inside a mattress which was left out as rubbish. The bin lorry which served the camp, unknown to its driver, took Hughes to freedom.

Hughes then became Arthur McAllister, toy salesman. Under this unlikely cover, he travelled around Belfast, meeting other senior Republicans and coordinating activities.

He knew it couldn't last. It didn't. He was arrested again,

convicted of possession of firearms and explosives, and sentenced to 15 years. He was sent back to Long Kesh. The process of criminalisation had now begun: the H-Blocks were opened in 1976. In 1977, following the release of Gerry Adams, Hughes became OC (officer commanding) of the Republican prisoners. When he was moved from the old, POW-style compounds to the new jail, he refused, as others had also done, to don the prison uniform.

The blanket protest gave way to the dirty protest. Still there was no sign of special category status being reinstated. In the autumn of 1980, Hughes decided the only option was hunger strike. On 27 October 1980, he refused food, as did six other prisoners.

"The first day I went on hunger strike, I was still in this shitty cell. But I remember thinking to myself that night, 'the cell doesn't look that bad.' Because that is the day you start to die. After a while you can actually smell your body wasting away."

By 18 December, negotiations were at a critical point. But Seán McKenna, one of the hunger strikers, was close to death. Believing that the prisoners' demands had been met, Hughes called the strike off. He still holds the view that the prison authorities then sabotaged the agreement.

A second hunger strike started. Ten men died. In the years after their deaths, most of their demands were conceded. Hughes was released from the H-Blocks in 1986, when he once again became active in the Republican movement.

The trauma of the period left a deep mark: "I blamed myself for years," Hughes said. "I used to believe that if I had let Seán die, that would have ended it, which would have stopped 10 men dying. During one period I was almost at the point of jumping off a bridge."

Hughes feels that the apparent abandonment of traditional

Republican objectives by the current leadership casts a shadow over the sacrifices made by him and others: "I don't think it's been worth it," he said. "If someone had told me 20 years ago, you're going to go to jail, you're going to get tortured, you're going to go on hunger strike, you're going to watch loads of men dying to get this—I'd have told them to forget it."

So much for the past. Where does Brendan Hughes think Republicanism should go from here? He is unequivocal about the fact that a return to armed struggle is not an option. "The most important thing at the moment is truth. The next most important thing is that people should be allowed free speech. The third objective is to force Republicanism to broaden the base of debate," he said.

Hughes tries to keep his disagreements with the current leadership on an ideological level, but it is impossible to expunge personal factors from the equation. If one wanted evidence that the personal really is political, Republicanism provides it. It's there in Hughes' own words when he talks of the "major problems" encountered by people trying to come to terms with the suffering they endured (or inflicted) during the conflict.

"There are many people who have gone through this whole struggle and have gone off their heads. Kieran Nugent, one of the first blanket men, finished up with people calling him a water rat, drinking wine at the side of a river. Loads of others have just died off," he said.

There is one note of personal bitterness sounded by Hughes, too. It goes back once again to ties of friendship. It goes back to Gerry Adams. Hughes believes that eventually his old comrade was using him only to further his (Adams') own agenda.

He recalled one period in the 1980s: "I was being trailed all over the country with him at that point. He was building up an electoral base. But I didn't know that. I was just Brendan

Hughes, the famous 'Darkie' Hughes who had escaped from jail and who'd been on hunger strike. My reputation was being used."

Adams and Hughes last met about three months ago. It wasn't a pleasant experience: "He was asking me questions about my getting publicity, talking about the 'Armani Suit Brigade' and so on. And he was saying things about the people I was associating with—that I had got myself into bad company and I should get myself out of it. It was an attempt to censor me through friendship. But it was so ridiculous! If Gerry had said that to me 20 years ago, I'd have fucked him a right!"

Yet, for all that, an old black and white photograph still hangs in Hughes' living room. Two men. Long hair in a Long Kesh cage. Big smiles. Arms around each other. Brothers-in-arms. Gerry Adams and Brendan Hughes. "The reason I keep that there is it reminds me what it used to be like," said Hughes. "We were 100% into it. One hundred percent."

BRENDAN HUGHES ON THE 20TH ANNIVERSARY OF THE HUNGER STRIKES

25 January 2001

"The Hunger Strikes—20 Years On, Where Are We Now?"

Thursday, 25 January 2001

ATGWU Hall, Dublin

Transcript, IRWG PUBLIC MEETING

After that last speaker, I was prepared to walk out—I don't know how I am going to beat that. Listen, we are a bit stuck for time and I could ramble on here for a long time on the jail situation but there is a few important points I want to make.

Briefly, I will give a bit of history on where I came from. I was born into a working class background, a socialist background, and became a member of the IRA, and went to jail, escaped from jail, went back into jail, became part of the prison protest. In 1972, there was a truce and the IRA asked for the British to give a declaration of intent to withdraw—and that would end the war. Two weeks later it was obvious the British were not coming across with that. The end of 1974/75 another ceasefire was called, this time it was a long drawn out ceasefire and the intentions of the British at that time was to get the IRA involved in a long drawn out ceasefire, and an attempt to normalise the situation, criminalise the situation and to pacify the situation. That basically meant to get the British troops off the street, the RUC back onto the street and put Republicans in jail. That they done.

In 1974/75/76, I was in the cages of Long Kesh and soon became OC in the cages of Long Kesh. In 1978 it was decided that I was no longer a political prisoner and on a morning in January 1978 I was negotiating with the governor and he called me "Mr. Hughes" or "OC." That afternoon I was taken out, brought to the H-Blocks of Long Kesh, and stripped, given a blanket and thrown into a cell. That was part of the criminalisation policy that the British government employed at that time. The intention was to turn me into a nice law-abiding criminal.

At that time the British believed that they had the struggle beaten - they refused to give a declaration of intent to withdraw, they refused to agree for the Irish people to come to their own conclusions of what sort of democracy, what sort of social democracy, we wanted here. The intentions from the war when I first got involved was to bring about a 32-county democratic *Socialist* Republic.

By 1980 we had been on the blanket protest for over four years and the brutality that took place there is just so undescribable. I mean we were locked in the cells 24 hours a day, we were starved, we were beaten, we went through the white light torture treatment at night—when the lights was left on. In the winter the heating was turned off, in the summer the heating was turned on. Men were taken out and beaten. They introduced the wing shifts, where a whole series, thirty men at a time—not all at one time, one man at a time, but thirty men on a wing—were taken out individually, beaten and thrown into another wing.

By 1980 we decided on the Hunger Strike, because we needed to end this protest, we needed to bring this to an end. There was so much suffering and so much agony. On the outside what was taking place was that the Republican Movement had rebuilt. This time more politically aware than they were before 1975. On the streets there were mass protest on behalf—there wasn't mass protests actually—not until the Hunger Strikes. The common phrase in the H-Blocks at that time was: "Does anyone care? Does anyone know?" The first Hunger Strike was called and it wasn't long before the world knew, and we called on the world for support, to support our five demands.

The Hunger Strike which I was involved in, myself and Bobby decided—Bobby Sands—we decided to call the Hunger Strike. Tommy was on the Hunger Strike with me. We negotiated what we believed was the settlement of that Hunger Strike.

I don't know if anyone here has any experience of a hunger strike, but it is an agonising, torturous, smelly way to die. I remember the first thought I had the first day I was on hunger strike. I was lying in a shitty cell, on a piece of mattress, on a wet floor, cold, hungry—and I'd been that way for over three years. But the first day I went on hunger strike was the day I looked back at yesterday and thought "well, that wasn't too bad." I mean this is the day you start to die. Yesterday I could have lived for a year, two years, three years, I could have stuck it for that length of time. But today is hell, today is the day you die.

When you go on hunger strike, if you have any excess fat on your body, your body will eat it. Once the excess fat is gone, and believe me there wasn't too many fat men in the H-Blocks of Long Kesh, it then eats at the muscle and your muscles starts to go. Once all the muscle is gone all that is left is flesh and bone. The body is a fantastic machine, it will keep itself alive. So the next thing to go is the brain. Your body starts to live off your brain, it takes the glucose from your brain. Once that starts that's the critical period. That's when your eyesight starts to go, your smell, all your senses start to go. Then you go into a coma. Then you die. Agonisingly, an agonising death. And an agonising death for a family member, a parent, a mother, to sit and have to watch this. That is the reality of hunger strike.

We believed that we had settled the first Hunger Strike. It turned out that we were betrayed in that settlement and that led to the second Hunger Strike. Now the second Hunger Strike, as you all know, cost ten men their lives. Ten men died on it. The Hunger Strikes ended. Now I don't want to get in too deeply into that, just keep it brief because I think the next few points are the most important points that I am trying to make.

The Hunger Strike is so important to the struggle. It was part of the struggle, part of our struggle to bring about a 32-county democratic socialist Republic. But to be honest with you the day I called the Hunger Strike was the day to end the prison protest. That was the main decision, to end the prison protest, to end the struggle in the jails.

The struggle then went on until the next major development, which was the Hume/Adams document. Now I don't know if any of you have read the Hume/Adams document, but I certainly haven't read it and I've searched for it, looked for it, but I've never come across the Hume/Adams document. If anyone has it, would they please give me it, because I have never come across it. The Hume/Adams document went on to the thing we now call the Good Friday Agreement.

Now I went to jail, spent the last thirty years of my life, trying to bring down an unjust, undemocratic, immoral, corrupt, sectarian statelet set up by the British. The Good Friday Agreement has brought about that same state, the thirty year struggle did not end the injustice of that statelet. We still have the RUC. The slogans were on the walls "Disband the RUC," then it became "Reform the RUC." Some time ago they brought a discredited conservative politician here to sort out the policing problem—the "policing problem." The new in word, by the way, with the RUC now is "transist," they are "transisting." So the next slogan goes on the wall is that the "RUC are transisting," into what I don't know, but they are no longer to be disbanded.

Stormont is still there, but it is a Stormont with Republicans in it. Stormont has not changed. The whole apparatus of the Stormont regime is still there, it is still controlled by the British, it is still unjust, it is still cruel. The RUC is still there. The whole civil service are still there, the same civil servants who controlled the shoot-to-kill policy, who controlled the plastic bullets, who controlled the H-Blocks of Long Kesh, who took responsibility for ten men dying. It is all still there. But, saviour of saviours, we have two Sinn Féin ministers there, who happen to close hospitals.

The sad thing about all this is that the British set this up. This is the British answer to the Republican problem in Ireland. It's a British solution, it's not an Irish solution. It's not a solution that we have control of. There are people up there and the British ministers are handing money out. But the whole thing is built on sand. First of all the statelet still exists. Secondly, whenever Tony Blair, or whoever comes after him, decides—or the Unionists decide—to walk out, the Good Friday Agreement is finished. It's all finished. So the whole thing is built on sand. The unfortunate thing about it is that there are people who actually believe that we have a settlement, that we have a settlement to our problem, to your problem, to my problem, to everybody's problem in Ireland. And I don't believe that.

I was in London a few weeks ago. I was asked over by a group of people, the Kurds and the Turkish people, who are in Turkish prisons. Why I was there was they asked Sinn Féin for support. Thirty-two people have died, twelve of them hunger strikers in Turkish jails. Sinn Féin's response to these people was "we do not get involved in the internal politics of another country." God help us all. That's what the response was "we do not get involved in the internal politics of another country." To me that is a total betrayal.

On the Falls Road, the heart of the resistance struggle in Ireland to bring about a socialist republic, we have employers who are paying women £2 an hour, who are paying men £20 a day for working on building sites in all types of weather with no security that they will have a job tomorrow morning. I know men who went in to work for a day and because the people did not like their face they were sacked. They were sacked because the person who was employing did not like their face. These same people are employing a lot of ex-prisoners, a lot of these people done 10, 15, 20 years in prison. These same people, these rogue builders, are now millionaires who own five bars on the Falls Road. These are the same people that built the new Sinn Féin office, with slave labour. The new Sinn Féin office on the Falls Road, a real luxury building; and the local paper, the Andytown News, these same people built that. These are the people who are paying men £20 a day and who are abusing them and sacking them and it's so totally unbelievable and so disgusting, but that's what they are getting away with.

Now it took me a long time within the Republican Movement, if you are in a movement for over thirty years you have a certain amount of loyalty to it. When the Good Friday Agreement was agreed upon I had my doubts, I had my reservations. But I stayed there for a long time, I stayed there for far too long while people like Tommy McKearney and Anthony McIntyre were sticking their necks out. Until I began to see and open my eyes and see what was going on. The best friend I had all my life was Gerry Adams. This isn't anything personal against Gerry Adams, although I have been accused of it, of mounting a personal campaign against Gerry Adams. I am not. Gerry Adams happens to wear an Armani suit, I attack everybody in Sinn Féin who wears Armani suits, because the working class doesn't have them.

So I joined the Republican Writers Group and began to write. I began to write about the excesses of these rogue builders. I began to write about an old Republican, who I knew all my life, who the IRA and Sinn Féin evicted out of his house, because the British government was offering £50,000 of a grant to Sinn Féin open it as drop-in centre for prisoners. I was an ex-prisoner and I'd have been saying to them, "fuck your fifty thousand, the Republican is more important to me than fifty thousand pounds."

So really what we are doing, and it wasn't easy for people like us to do this. I mean we have lost so-called friends. I wouldn't say we have lost comrades, because you don't lose a comrade unless he dies, or she dies. We have lost so-called friends because of our actions and, as I say, it is not easy to do what we do. Myself and Anthony travelled all over, we went to meet the families of the hunger strikers from London. We were arrested on the way in and probably will be arrested again. They won't let us in to America. What we are trying to do is cause a debate. We have an alternative to the Good Friday Agreement, we have an alternative to the British settlement in Ireland. We have it, the people have it. It has to be a socialist alternative, it has to be a Republican alternative. That's what we are trying to do. We are trying to start a great debate, we have one organised in Belfast next week and I hope to God it is as well attended as this, I somehow doubt it, but I hope it is.

To end I want to thank you all for coming and I really appreciate you listening to me. Thanks very much.

WHAT OF THE WORKING PEOPLE?

Spring 2001

You have not converted a man because you have silenced him.
—John Morley

ORIGINALLY PUBLISHED IN *THE OTHER VIEW*

So, what of the working person in our new set up in the six counties? We are in the process of seeing "our" police force being dry-cleaned. We are in the process of seeing "our" Stormont being whitewashed. We are in the process of seeing "our" Republican Movement shedding its skin. We are certainly not in any process of seeing the conditions of the workers being improved. Women are still being forced to work for £2 an hour; men for £20 a day. What has the Good Friday Agreement done for the working class people? As a Republican, as far as I can see—nothing!

For the working people the GFA may as well mean "Got Feck All." It has delivered absolutely nothing. What should the Republican Movement be doing for working people? Absolutely everything. The rogue builders that plague and prey on working class Republican communities should not be allowed to treat workers as slaves—in work one day and out the next because the boss takes a dislike to you or may resent the fact that you do not drink your wages in the bar that he owns and in which he pays you. He can quite easily find some other wretched soul who feels compelled out of poverty to work for less than the £20 a day he gives you. Whatever happened to the old adage of a "fair day's work for a fair day's pay"?

It seems to me that after thirty years of struggling we are still facing repression—by the British, by our so-called "own people." If after thirty years of grueling war, death and hunger, we end up with a British administered six-county state alongside a 26-county republic, both of which exploit and repress working people, then it has all been in vain. Any internal arrangement (and it is an arrangement for the prosperous not a solution for the poor) or for that matter a thirty-two county arrangement that leaves the condition of working people untouched was simply not worth thirty years of war and death.

Do the Unionist communities have a similar experience? How are their ex-prisoners treated? Would the PUP (Progressive Unionist Party), which claims to be radical and for the working man and woman, allow those who are nothing better than the slum landlords of the building industry to build their party offices with a grossly underpaid workforce who are not allowed to be unionised? How do those who claim to be socialist within the Unionist community resist such exploitation? If there is to be a meaningful debate between Republicanism and loyalism, let it begin there rather than with the waffle and nonsense about flags that passes for dialogue up at Stormont.

James Connolly was right when he said Ireland without its people meant nothing to him. In all honesty, if it were the only way to avoid exploitation and the rule of poverty creators, and if such a thing were possible, I would prefer a six-county democratic socialist republic where the workers would have control of their own destiny, the right to work and security of employment. A republic where it is a crime to exploit workers and where the employment of rogue builders would be banned by sheer morality never mind the law.

In other words a society where there is...

JUSTICE.

TELLING RONNIE FLANAGAN FIRST

27 March 2001

How does Ronnie Flanagan know before we do? He now tells us that there is about to be a second round of decommissioning. Who told him that the IRA were poised to destroy more weapons? Who gives the IRA permission to destroy or hand over guns to the British or their friends? I certainly did not. I was never even asked what I thought.

The British still occupy this country. The British still control us. And while they do no one has the right to hand over or destroy weapons to please the British. Weapons belong to Republicans. They do not belong to Stormont politicians. We fought and died with those hard-won weapons. We went to jail for holding onto them. People were executed for informing on them. And now the Sinn Féin leadership are destroying them to meet the enemy demands. Our only means of defence are surrendered. Nationalists are being attacked daily. Why not be honest and admit defeat? No, why not be honest and admit surrender?

Liam Mellows always warned Republicans about those people who get power solely for the privileges that power brings. To my friends who ask why I speak out this is the reason. A love of people, a love of justice, a love of truth—and a hatred of power that gives privilege to the few and abuse to the many.

THE REAL MEANING OF THE G.F.A.

8 October 2001

The truth is not simply what you think it is;
it is also the circumstances in which it is said,
and to whom, why, and how it is said.
—Václav Havel

For almost thirty years the Republican Movement fought a war against the British to remove them from Ireland and establish a thirty-two county democratic socialist republic. We wanted control of the wealth in this country to rest with those who created it—working men and women.

In a bid to prevent any such thing taking place armed sectarian groups emerged—quite often under the direction of the British who made use of the sectarian divide for their own strategic ends. Many people died as a result, others were injured or imprisoned. Almost exclusively, those who suffered were from working class backgrounds both here and in Britain.

Thirty years on, despite our best efforts the sectarian divide still exists. Some say it is beginning to break down now that we have the Good Friday Agreement and a cross community executive at Stormont; that things at long last will begin to look better for the working class. Jolly good show—Hurrah or what old boy?

There is a coming together alright. But after reading the Unionist Fred Cobain in last week's Irish News it is not difficult to see how the dice is loaded in favour of the rich. He termed the whole sorry charade up at Stormont a middle class government for a middle class people.

I was particularly interested in one aspect of Mr. Cobain's assessment. He claimed that 600 people would die over the course of the next year as a result of poor heating in their homes. The poor and handicapped, be they Catholic, Protestant, Jew, Dissenter are all invited by her majesty's government at Stormont to come together and huddle as a means of keeping warm. We can rest assured that no one at Stormont will die due to a lack of heat. They might explode due to overeating.

A number of years ago I stood on a freezing site in West Belfast interviewing working class people about a rogue-building firm giving them a bad deal. One of the firms worker's pointed out that at the same time as the Tory Government had introduced VAT on fuel this firm was cutting the required statutory amount of housing insulation by half. In other words the poor were being told by the ruling class that they would pay more for their heat and when they eventually scraped together the money for it, it would vanish out the roof twice as quickly because of profit mad builders. Their powerful friends ensured that the findings were never published.

Fred Cobain is to be commended for speaking out and allowing us to see that in the years since that day when I stood on the site, little has really changed. Same old ship, just some different hands at the wheel. Now we are beginning to understand

what the GFA really means. For working class Protestants and
Catholics: *Got F— All.*

UNDER THE FOOT OF THE MOUNTAIN
Winter 2002

I had a walk down the Grosvenor Road yesterday to see my sister, to the place I was born, to the place my father brought up six children on his own, to a place I spent almost four years on the run, a place where we fought the B Specials, RUC, British Army, British Intelligence, and undercover killers. A place where poor people left their front and back doors open. A place where you had to get to know every yard wall in the event of a Brit army raid. A place where we had great hopes of our Republic.

But it had all changed. I saw nice new houses. No more yard walls; one way in and one way out. Most of the old people who had fed and looked after us, gone, dead and buried. The old people's home knocked down, leaving a wide open space, being prepared for the next rogue builder to come in and build some cheap houses for the poor people of this area. But what struck me was the view the place had left for us to see and wonder at.

Towering above the small and neat houses, like two giants protecting those who can afford entry into their bellies; reminding us that we are in the place we belong. The giants even have their names boldly written across their foreheads—Europa and Russell Court. It reminds me of a time I sailed into Cape Town on a merchant ship. The imposing table top mountain towering above—beautiful sight. A sight that cried out for you to come up and see.

That is, until you step off the ship and witness the ugly feet of this mountain. The poor, the hungry, the poverty this great beauty hides. Before leaving the ship we are told to stay away from the shantytowns, and especially stay away from "District 6" as I'm sure many visitors to our Europa are told when they arrive in Belfast. Of course many things have changed in South Africa, many things have changed in the North. But have they?

Yes, for some! But for the majority of people, poor people, here and in South Africa, nothing much has changed. We still have the rogue employer, maybe a different colour, maybe a different religion. We are allowed to climb the mountain but few can afford to do so. Few people living under the shadow of the Europa can afford to spend one night in its belly.

We spend billions of pounds each year on weapons. Each year millions of children die both from hunger, and from the weapons we spend billions on. More often than not whether in Western Europe, South Africa or Palestine the biggest rogue employers are the people tasked with governing us.

WHO ARE THE TERRORISTS?

17 January 2002

Let everyone sweep in front of his own door,
and the whole world will be clean.
—Johann Wolfgang von Goethe

A warning is given. A bomb goes off in Belfast. It was not meant to kill anyone. Right or wrong for planting it, to kill people was not the objective. This all raises questions of who is right? Who is wrong? What is right? What is wrong? The war is right—or so it seems. Who wins decides. The winner makes the judgement. In the cold light of day we know that the winner has the power to decide.

If Hitler had won the Second World War—thankfully he did not—questions and answers about rights and wrongs would have been viewed very differently from how they are today. From where we sit at the bottom of society's social ladder, it seems it is our lot to live, fight, die. "Such is life" as Ned Kelly would have said. But then he didn't take it lying down and ended up being called a terrorist. As was Fidel Castro. Gerry Adams was called a terrorist and so was Archbishop Makarios.

What we get called by the establishment in no way affects the truth. I was called a terrorist. I never saw myself as one. I did not invade someone else's country—like my accusers. I did not kill kids—like my accusers. I did not kill innocent people—like my accusers. And they who accused the most, the British Government, murdered and tortured all with the approval of the British people. They allowed it to happen. Rather than search further they believed the BBC or ITV.

Today the terrorist is Bin Laden. Who gave him the weapons and training? It was not the poor people of the USA. It was not the "terrorists" from Ireland. It was the Government of the USA. Why is he a terrorist for using the weapons and training the American Government provided him with when the Government of Israel is not despite using the same weapons and training to kill kids in Palestine? Why is the Turkish Government, so busy murdering prisoners and their families, not terrorists when it too uses the same weapons and training?

Is the real terrorist really those young men and women who grew up in the Palestinian refugee camps and strap a bomb to their own bodies in a cry for justice? Yes—but only if you believe the BBC. Dig a bit deeper and a different truth might come to light. And then we may be closer to solving real problems.

OFF WITH THEIR BEARDS

17 January 2002

In the phraseology of politics, a party too indifferent to the sorrow and sufferings of humanity to raise its voice in protest, is a moderate, practical party; whilst a party totally indifferent to the personality of leaders, or questions of leadership, but not to enthusiasm on every question affecting the well-being of the toiling masses, is an extreme, a dangerous party.

—James Connolly

We learned this week that the Yanks had shaved off the beards of their Taliban prisoners. Not a new tactic. The Brits did it with us in the H-Blocks in 1978. Why? The blanket protest, no-wash, no shaving was a way in which we could highlight our case to the wider world that we were not criminals. We lay unwashed, we grew long beards, we put our own shit on the walls of the cells. These extraordinary lengths we went to in order to make ourselves heard over and above the British imposed silence—we were not criminals. When that was not enough we went further and ten men died, bringing the attention of the world to Ireland and shattering the British myth.

Getting rid of our beards had proved useless. As against the

Taliban in Guantanamo Bay today it was an exercise in power. It was merely to degrade and let us know they were the boss and could do as they wanted with us—no one could stop them. But they failed. They were only the boss of the jail—never our minds. They could not persuade us to think that we were criminal and we persuaded the world that we were not.

Elsewhere in the world today prisoners still fight against oppressive regimes. At the time of writing 82 men and women have died as a result of hunger strike activity in Turkey. The white Anglo-Saxons of the so-called civilised world in its smugness ignores them or worse, supports the regime that kills them. As each death is announced we hear silence from our own political establishment. They can make plenty of noise and be heard when they are demanding pay rises for themselves. Justice for Turkish prisoners—well that is another thing. Why make noise about them? It is easier to dismiss them as fanatical or fundamentalist—anything but come out on their behalf. Yet these people are not fascist or dictatorial. Whatever we think of their methods they are socialists fighting for the rights of man—for human freedom.

I would remind our political establishment or at least those who term themselves radical within it that it is the ordinary people of Palestine and Turkey who are suffering. Do not forget the poor of either country. Do not fool yourselves into thinking that because you have a foot in the door of Stormont that you have a foothold on power and that it is better to stay silent when justice demands otherwise rather than lose that power. In this world real power lies with the men with no beards—for us that means those at No. 10 in London.

WHO IS STILL HERE?

22 January 2002

In revolution there are two types of people:
those who make it and those who profit from it.
—Napoleon I

It is easy to lift a gun. It is even easy to fire it. When you see the body of a 17-18 year old it is not so easy.

We were young. They were young too. The British Government sent them onto the streets of Belfast. The IRA sent us out to oppose them. I took no pleasure seeing a young Englishman lying on the street. But I admit to taking pleasure from taking on the might of the British Empire.

Most of the kids who died here knew nothing of why they were here. The bulk of them came from poor working class families just like our own. I remember one time in McDonnell Street a young British soldier had been left behind by his foot patrol. He was only 18. I was not at the scene but soon received word that the IRA had captured a British soldier and were holding him captive. In those days we did not have radio communication. By the time I arrived at McDonnell Street the 18 year old soldier was already dead. He had been shot dead by a 17 year old IRA volunteer. I regret to this day that I was unable to stop his death.

We had no desire to kill kids whether in uniform or not. But it was kids who fought this war on both the British and Irish sides. I was never filled with hatred for other human beings. I did not hate the English people. I hated what the British Government did to my country.

Today I left my flat which is situated near the top of the high rise complex in which I live. When I reached the ground floor I met three armed British soldiers waiting to take over the lift. No one is allowed to use our lift when the British soldiers change guard. But the lift was put there for the residents not an occupying army.

It is not easy to swallow it. If you live in London or New York, could you feel indifferent, if you were to walk out of your home to be confronted by a number of armed foreigners who insist on telling you what you may and may not do? I don't think so.

As I walked up the Falls and past the commemorative garden built to honour the dead volunteers who had given their lives resisting the repression inflicted by the British Army I thought to myself that despite all the promises and new arrangements, the British hadn't gone away, you know.

THEY THINK IT'S ALL OVER

4 February 2002

In any great organization
it is far, far safer
to be wrong with the majority
than to be right alone.
—John Kenneth Galbraith

If it is all over what was it for? Do we have freedom? Not the type I fought for. Did we get rid of oppression? Not the type I fought against. Did we change fundamental economic and social structures or did we change those who would run the same old ones? Does the working class get anything out of this deal? If so why then is Sinn Féin claiming that the working class in the Falls Road still live in one of the poorest areas in Europe? Did the deal rid us of the rogue employers and greedy financiers who exploit our squalor like cockroaches? Did Republicans in the poor communities get anything out of this deal? How can we even begin to discuss this openly if those who think we get nothing can only say so at the risk of being hounded and vilified?

I remember always being impressed by Liam Mellows when he said people get into positions of power and then will do almost anything to hold on to that power because of the privilege power brings them. Why should such power be used to give privilege to rogue employers and others who exploit the poor in our communities? Is it because it brings mutual reward?

How can the use of power be justified if it fails to protect those employed by rogue businesses and instead gives contracts to those businesses? Maybe we were all naive in striving for such principled goals. But I don't think so. I just think we were right. Rather than being naive we were conned.

The ruling class still rules and the working class still works and the gap between the two is as bad as ever. Not only are the Brits still here but also are poverty, corruption, inequality, censorship and repression. How things change in order to stay the same. Can it really ever be all over when this is all we have to show for our efforts?

HITLER SPEAKING HEBREW

7 April 2002

The problems that exist in the world can't be solved
by the same type of thinking that caused them.
—Albert Einstein

Yesterday morning my door sounded as if it was about to crash in. The blattering accompanied by shouting through the small letterbox was frantic. It was just as well I had asked a friend to give me a wake up call. I had volunteered to drive the minibus to Dublin at the request of the Ireland Palestine Solidarity Committee. And I had almost slept in. But like everything else in these circumstances where the downtrodden are resisting, moral obligation and a sense of solidarity kick in and I always manage to make it and give my support.

A door being battered and hammered always reminds me of British Army raids. I felt relieved that it was just a friend doing the hammering. My thoughts drifted to those in occupied Palestine hearing similar noise followed by the voices of fascist Israeli soldiers in jackboots, then gunfire. In the wake of the visit, a child or another loved one dead. I would make it to Dublin even if I had to walk.

Things in Palestine have got so bad that even the Pope has condemned the Israeli government. But the thought crossed my mind that this was more to do with the fact that with nowhere else to escape the murderous Israeli assault the Palestinians were seeking refuge in churches. Had the Vatican conducted another sordid deal with fascism for which it is renowned—shoot all you want but not if they are on our property?

In prison I read books about the Warsaw Ghetto. *Mila 18* by Leon Uris gripped me because it was a story about resistance against odds that could not be overcome. But the alternative for the Jewish was to let the Nazi fascists march them off to the gas chambers. I admired those young Jewish fighters who went to their deaths fighting rather than pleading with a presumed human decency that simply did not exist. Some children as young as six crawled through the sewers of the ghetto to bring back food to keep their families alive. It went on for a long time. Each day as they began their descent into the sewer they must have realised that it could be their last—and for the majority it was. The Nazis rounded them up and murdered them for feeding their families. Other kids had to lie in secret hiding places from where they could watch helplessly as their mothers, fathers, brothers and sisters were herded off to death in the concentration camps.

I was not yet born when all this was taking place. But watching events in Palestine today I can see at first hand what it was like for those brave Jewish people in the Warsaw Ghetto. Innocent people under fascist and racist attack. And yet they resist. When we watch this we know that Hitler never really died but is on the march having donned the mask of those he sought to exterminate. He is writing the hated number on the arms of the Palestinians. What genocide has he planned for the Ramallah Ghetto?

And we know just how easy it can be to inflict such genocide when there are so many prepared to turn a blind eye. Nazi Germany went as far as it did because of blind eyes and cowardly silence. Do not let on you are unaware of what is happening. The spectre of Israeli racism is massacring the Palestinians. Do no give your children cause to condemn you for your indifference. Speak out and demand the end to the Israeli occupation of Palestine now.

TRUST YOUR LEADERS?

8 April 2002

If you love wealth better than liberty, the tranquility of servitude better than the animating contest of freedom, go home from us in peace. We ask not your counsels or your arms. Crouch down and lick the hands which feed you. May your chains set lightly upon you, and may posterity forget that you were our countrymen.

—Samuel Adams

James Connolly, in 1915, wrote a sarcastic article titled "Trust Your Leaders!" In it he claimed that, "in Ireland we have ever seized upon mediocrities and made them leaders." He could just as easily have been writing about 2002 rather than 1915. How can you trust leaders who endlessly tell you one thing and do the opposite?

Taking the gun out of Irish politics is a joke. It is a sick joke because the only gun being taken out is the Republican gun. Now that another bunch of weapons has been decommissioned I feel for all those poor people who never made it to the TV studios, who never graced foreign capitals, who lived in tiny homes with their door always open as we hid our guns in their cupboards, under their beds, in their drawers and beneath their floorboards. The anonymous poor, the real heroes and heroines of this struggle.

We are occupied and have more right to have weapons than those who occupy us. Yet the British demand that we and not they give up guns. Imagine England invaded by the Nazis and the appeasers advised the English people to "destroy your weapons. The Nazis insist on it." Would you? I am not comparing the English people to the Nazis but the point is that we in Ireland have been invaded by armed English soldiers intent on murdering, torturing and jailing a civilian population. Why should we—the victims in all of this—hand over or allow the weapons to be destroyed? Those weapons were used not to invade but to defend our communities and to obtain Irish freedom.

I can see what has happened today as nothing other than surrender. But not everybody surrenders. One thing holds true in all of this and that is Ireland is occupied by Britain and for as long as that remains there will always be Irish people who will resist that occupation. Handing over or destroying weapons in order to accept British rule in Ireland is neglecting our own responsibility and passing it on to another generation.

And what social conditions will a new generation face? Tony Blair has proclaimed New Labour. Republicans have proclaimed New Sinn Féin. All new waffle. There is not much that I can see that separates them. What then about something really new? What about new socialism? A socialism that would ignore the tripe talkers and their vanguard party nonsense? One thing that is not new is the working class. It is as old as capitalism itself. They are still being exploited, maltreated, forced to work for bad pay on unhealthy sites with poor safety regulations. Could someone please tell me where a worker's wage packet is fatter than a politician's? Or where oppression of the working class is not planned? It is not in Stormont, Leinster House or

Westminster. They all love the workers alright as long as they can keep them working for buttons.

Take the gun out of Irish politics—maybe. But not at the command of those in the above three parliaments. As long as there is injustice the gun will always be there. And if we really want to take it out why not give it to the Palestinians? And who will have the cheek to tell us that they do not need it?

WHO GUARDS THE GUARDS?

10 April 2002

It is only circumstances and environment that make burglars, therefore anybody is liable to be one.

I don't quite know how I have managed to escape myself.

—Mark Twain

Who robbed Castlereagh? The IRA? UVF? UDA? RUC top brass? MI5? CID? Special Branch? Or is it a mix of them all? A bit of this and a bit of that and we the public can take our pick? Why not throw a few more into the hat such as FRU, the RIR or even what passes for the KGB these days? They are all still there—none have gone away you know.

I apologise for all the questions even if they do have a purpose—just as those who robbed Castlereagh surely did. And what could that be? Clearly there is somebody who does not want us to know what is going on. But that is nothing new in this place. If we are the most politically informed population in Western Europe, as we are sometimes told, I don't know how—because there is never anybody willing to tell us anything. The ordinary people on the ground have to sit like spectators at a football match watching the ball go back and forward and are expected to cheer if one crowd score in the blame game by making it appear that the other side are guilty. Anyway we are none the wiser now three weeks after it all happened.

I was in Castlereagh—not on St Patrick's Day. I just want to make that clear before the cops come booting my door in as they have with so many others. It was always the last place in the world I wanted to be, or would want to go back to, even if it was for a bit of thieving. On paper it is a holding centre but for those of us who suffered in the place it was a torture chamber—and you knew you were there. Whoever did it must have had great courage—Republicans have plenty of that. Or, and more believable, they did not need courage as they knew they were coming out again and alive. Now, who would that be, desk sergeant?

Whoever did it, one thing is for sure, nobody in these areas will get a pay rise because of it.

THE PUTRID SMELL OF THE MIDDLE CLASS

18 April 2002

I sit on a man's back choking him and making him carry me, and yet assure myself and others that I am sorry for him and wish to lighten his load by all possible means—except by getting off his back.

—Leo Tolstoy

I used to watch them. They came and they went. The collar and tie. The priest, the probation officer, the so-called social worker. Through the broken window or grill from my stinking cell I watched them pass, the clean smell of their after shave wafting across and into my nostrils. I liked the scent but not the people bearing it. I wanted it but I did not want to change places with them. I was with the poor—as unwashed as I was—of Belfast and Derry estates, Tyrone, and South Armagh villages. A better class of people. Despite no after-shave they even smelt better too. For years I never could figure out why.

There was no envy on my part for those "Christian" people of so-called good intent. I would watch as they walked, ignoring me and the "bad" people. Their smug sense of self-satisfaction adding a bounce to their step. Hypocrites that they were they could walk out smiling after having witnessed another beating, a kid being tortured, starved, beaten and degraded. And they walked but never talked. Their comfortable existence kept them quiet.

Ten men died because people like that did nothing. Because they stayed silent ten men had to speak in the only way they could in order to make the world listen. The boys on hunger strike were no saints—we can be grateful for that. If being saintly meant walking up the H-Block yard with your nose in the air, indifferent to the misery just yards away, feigning some Christianity then sainthood was definitely not for us. It seemed to be anything but what Jesus Christ stood for. But then he wasn't saintly enough for them either so they done him in. Just as they did Bobby, Tom, Red Mick and the others in.

Of course, it was "suicide." People "took their own lives" and sinned against God their maker. Perhaps that eases the conscience for them as they sit in their big houses, looking out at their latest fancy car, tripping over the altar rails, collecting the next fat wage packet, buying the newest cologne.

Now when I think back to those days in the H-Blocks, I know why we smelt better than the "good" people. They carried the real stench—the rotten odour of middle class corruption.

THE TERRIFYING POWER OF LIFE AND DEATH

7 September 2002

How do you kill a child? For some people it seems quite easy—look at the Middle East today. There were times when I had the chance. I remember standing outside a shop in Leeson Street. A young British soldier was at the corner crying for his "mummy." I stood over him with a .45 aimed at his head. I could easily have physically pulled the trigger and sent him off to eternity. But morally and emotionally I was not able to end his life. He was a mere child, so frightened, out of his own country facing what his politicians and commanding officers told him were the "mad Irish." I could not shoot him. In a gun battle, at a distance, beyond the sound of his cries, where he had a soldier's chance I could have. But at that point the thing I felt it was my duty to kill—the soldier—had died within him. Now stood only a child whimpering in front of me.

I wonder where he is now. Is he alive with children of his own? Alive because the "mad Irish" were not all that mad and refrained from ending his life outside Greenwood's shop on Leeson Street. You lucky little bastard! And I am so glad. I just hope you did not grow into something hateful who would do to others what I refused to do to you. I hope not. I hope you are alive and living life to the full.

You came here at the direction of your leaders to invade our country. I had more reason to end your life than you ever had to take mine. I do not know you yet I know you so well. The two of us, working class guys thrown in against each other so that others could benefit. You were English and I was Irish—hardly reasons to kill each other.

Farewell British soldier. May you and your children live happy lives. I would like to see you again—but not in uniform.

IRA VOLUNTEER CHARLIE HUGHES AND THE COURAGE OF THE BRAVE

10 September 2002

I deliberately set out to write this article without using a bookie's pen. But the supposedly good pen I selected for this occasion was not so good after all. And so I am back to relying on old faithful—the little half-size blue pen from the bookies. Charlie Hughes would have had a laugh at that—"trust him" would have been his attitude. While he never took a drink he did enjoy the occasional flutter at the horses. I suppose horses run in the Hughes family. A matter of weeks ago we buried the well known Horsey Hughes. He was taken to his last resting place in a horse drawn carriage. The way to go Horsie. I'll be going that way too.

I guess these days, Charlie Hughes is just another name to so many people. He is dead 31 years and this city has moved on a lot since then. But to those who knew him, he will always rest in that little spot deep in our minds through the gates of which pass only the best. And Charlie was the best.

Charlie, with his infectious laugh and strong will, was the son of my aunt Bella who lived in Servia Street. It is now part of the area known as the Lower Falls. He was OC of D Company—the Dogs—the 2nd battalion of the Belfast Brigade. He was dedicated to the IRA and its goals. By joining the army he was following in a family tradition. Many of the Hughes family walked a similar path, although unfortunately for Charlie his path had already been marked out as the property of the reaper. It was he who brought me into the IRA.

When the events of 1969 caused the IRA to split, the choice for Charlie was straightforward. There was only one IRA and that was the IRA that fights. He quickly became OC of the Dogs. Throughout 1970 and early 1971 Republican resistance to the Northern State became more intense. In this very area, in one of its first major moves to slap down the nationalist people, the British imposed a curfew. With British troops on the streets doing the dirty work of Stormont, Charlie began to come into his own. With his powerful skills of leadership, he was a man that we all looked up to. His house was a hotbed of rebel activity. His mother Bella, was a constant and loyal source of support.

While the war was against the British, the split in the IRA had left a lot of bad feeling about. The Official IRA in the area could never forgive younger people like Charlie for snubbing it after it had deserted the people and left them at the mercy of orange and RUC mobs. The young looked to people like Billy McKee who had left the IRA but who had not left his people. Billy and others like him fought in defence of these areas. The Official IRA could not take the snub or the sneers of the people who took to painting the walls "IRA—I Ran Away."

After the split the Lower Falls had the largest concentration of Official IRA members in Belfast. Most of those had been there before the outbreak of sectarian and state violence in 1969. The Provisional IRA was small in the area but determined. The Officials had the bulk of the weaponry and in the area the majority of the support. Often Charlie and his comrades found that they were harassed and abused by the Official IRA, deeply resentful of any contender to their supposed throne. On occasions they were actually stopped and searched by the Official IRA. As if the British doing it was not bad enough. On one occasion the Officials captured two Provisional IRA volunteers and took them to one of their drinking clubs in Leeson Street where they proceeded to pistol-whip them. They were severely beaten. One D Company volunteer who witnessed the incident reported it to Charlie, who in turn referred matters up to Billy McKee and Proinsias Mac Airt.

The choices were clear. The Provisional IRA could either allow this reformist element to crush it on behalf of the British or it would stand up for itself. There was only ever one option, the latter. No one would refer to the Provisional IRA as "I Ran Away." The word came down from the leadership to all D Company volunteers to go into immediate stand-by mode and to open all arms dumps. A decision was taken by leadership to torch two drinking clubs run by the Official IRA. Throughout the night the small D Company numbers were reinforced by volunteers from other companies. The meeting point was none other than Charlie's house.

A number of hours passed and then the order came. The Burning Embers was to be made to live up to its name. It was located directly facing Charlie's house. The assembled volunteers prepared to move out. They did so reluctantly. None wanted to be involved in fighting other Republicans, but if the IRA was to survive to defend the districts and punish the British for their military offensive, there was no way that reformist Republicans, who wanted to go into the state apparatus rather than fight it, could be allowed to apply the jackboot.

The volunteers left Charlie's home and made their way to the Burning Embers. Upon entering they came across a party for Jim Sullivan, the Official IRA OC. The volunteers asked all present to leave in order to avoid injury. They declined. They were then ordered to leave. They refused. At that point Charlie gave the order to "burn it." But he told all the volunteers to throw their petrol bombs behind the bar and not anywhere near the customers. The purpose was to frighten them out rather than harm them physically. It succeeded.

Once the Burning Embers were well and truly on its way to becoming little other than embers the order was given for the Provisional IRA unit to move up to the Cracked Cup in Lesson Street, another of the Official IRA's drinking dens. But already alerted, the Official IRA were waiting to ambush the unit. A gun battle broke out and two volunteers were shot and injured. Shortly after this incident a ceasefire was agreed and the volunteers of the Provisional IRA dispersed to their billets while a strategy meeting was arranged to take place in Squire Maguire's house in Cyprus Street. Charlie and the brigade staff attended and it was agreed that all weapons would be put away overnight and that talks with the Official IRA would resume in the morning. Charlie was not convinced of the wisdom of putting the weapons away. And when the brigade staff members were leaving Squire's house he, as OC of the Dogs and feeling ultimately responsible for the safety of all volunteers in his area positioned himself behind a lamppost to give them cover. A shot rang out. The Official IRA had broken the agreement and IRA volunteer Charlie Hughes lay dead. He was the first fatality in what was to become a bout of feuds between the Officials and the Provisionals which broke out periodically right up until 1977.

Betrayed and murdered by reformists, the trail blazed by Charlie Hughes was one many young IRA volunteers followed inspired by his courage and commitment. Nearing death on hunger strike in the H-Blocks in 1980, his spirit was my food. He was never far away. I survived while he lies in the plot of the brave from where his inspiration reaches out to touch those of us who had the honour of knowing him.

PALESTINE AND IRAQ

16 September 2002

Iraq looks set to face a war waged upon it by America and its main ally the Brits. I have no doubt that Saddam Hussein is a brutal thug who deserves to go. But he is not on his own. George Bush would have us believe that that the war criminal Ariel Sharon is a man of peace. How much crap are we to plug into our ears and allow it to stop us hearing the cry of the innocent pounded by American bombs? Telling us that Sharon is a man of peace is like telling us Hitler was a humanitarian.

The war about to be fought is not about removing injustice. It is about putting some other bastard in to replace Saddam Hussein so long as he is a bastard that won't threaten US interests. How many more people will we in the West allow to die before this fact hits home? If something is right we should support it but where it is wrong we must oppose it. What is happening to the people of Palestine is wrong. What is about to happen to the people of Iraq is wrong. Saddam Hussein is a tyrant Mr. Bush but Ariel Sharon is no man of peace—how about taking some action against him?

Ten of my friends died during the hunger strike. They received much support from the Palestinians. They didn't even know us but they could identify with us. Have we paid them back in kind? I don't think so. We have watched the injustice inflicted upon them while our leaders have flirted with Washington. The Irish people need to speak out on the Palestinian question. They need to speak out against the US government who are about to bomb Iraq because while they bomb it Sharon will be sticking the boot into the Palestinians.

Justice is Truth. Injustice is a big lie. And the big lie facing us today is one that condemns Iraq and excuses Israel.

VOLUNTEER PATRICIA MCKAY

8 May 2003

Winding back the clock is something we can all do if we want to fool ourselves. Time moves on regardless of the clock. If it was just as simple to change things by fiddling with the hands of a clock who would not have a try? But as many of our comrades learned to their cost the hands of the clock can have fatal consequences. One wrong move when priming a bomb and setting the clock timer and that was it. Time stopped forever.

As I watch the turn political events have taken in recent years I think back to all those who lost their lives trying to move out of the time warp this society existed in. So many dead and so many casualties—for what? The miles I tramped at the funerals of those who died as a result of the war here would claim more than one pair of Horsey Hughes's boots. Many of them were decent, good, honest boys and girls who knew little of life other than its injustices, which they fought against.

A place, a comment, an event—it does not take much to bring a sad memory back of young people who should be here with us now, but instead lie up the road in their own silent place. Our local culture has it that the only volunteers who died were members of our own organisation, the Provisional IRA. But that is simply not true.

When I think of how myths develop I look back to 1972 when a gun battle took place in what is known as the Lower Falls. We fought the British Army all day—from corner to corner in the tight streets. Provisional IRA volunteers were not alone that day—members of the Official IRA were there too. One of those involved was a young Official IRA female volunteer. During the fighting I ended up in the same small house as her. The Brits had us pinned down with heavy gunfire from the direction of Conway Mill. She insisted on moving out and making a break for it. She was only 19 and I tried persuading her to hold on until a better chance presented itself. I knew her mother and father and wanted to do what was best for them and for her. My only regret at her being in the Official IRA was that I could not order her to sit tight. It was a different organisation and I had no control over its volunteers.

She walked out the door and the British Army shot her dead. "Such is life," Ned Kelly would have said. But I think it is more than that. Life should not have to be that way where our young die to resist injustice. She was just a kid—a kid in the Official IRA, like so many who were with me in the Provisional IRA. And so many kids went down the same path as she. A "wee Sticky," she was our comrade. A beautiful kid, Patricia McKay was her name. Although more than 30 years have passed since she lost her life, I have never forgotten her. She deserves to be honoured like every other volunteer from this community who lost their lives fighting the British Army. Whatever benefits we gained from this war, she as much as any other volunteer paid for them with her life's blood.

CHEATS

11 May 2003

Looking around me at a time when the politicians are never away from the television studios screaming "cheat" at each other, I feel a need to ask who are the cheats? Is it the employer? Is it the young mother who has to go out to work to keep her family going? Is it the men with maybe up to six kids who have to work in lousy conditions? It may be said that all these people function illegally but are they all cheats? The illegal behaviour of the employer is aimed at making profit. The illegal behaviour of the worker is aimed at keeping the family above the breadline—in other words, survival. More people have went to jail for seeking to keep their families safe than employers have ever went there for keeping them poor. How many employers in Belfast have been near a prison other than to build it? I don't know any.

If you have an employer who gives work to 20 "illegals" and enjoys a profit of £20,000 a month and ends up getting fined £5,000 in court, why let on you are surprised when he shouts "happy days—bring on the next 20"? He takes a chance because it is worth it. The "illegal" has to chance it because he or she has no choice—a hungry family quickly makes decisions for the breadwinner.

Belfast is full of greedy employers. It is even more full of poor people. But it is not just Belfast—look at Baghdad. Are the people there well off? But the bosses seem to be prosperous wherever they are. The lawmakers could do something about it. They could award a mandatory pay rise but they choose not to. The thought of having to go home without a pay packet is not something that keeps them awake at night.

Watching the news recently, I found it ironic that prison officers would be outside two prisons in the North protesting. The RUC were also coming under the spotlight—complaining about the way they are being treated. Two types of people whose wage packets were never less than bursting at the seams. Two sets of people who have suppressed any form of working class protest with the worst form of brutality. When I and many comrades and friends protested we were beaten and thrown naked into cells. And I recall saying to so many of those along with me that today it is our turn—when they finish with us they will turn on others. For that reason we will never see the screws or Special Branch having to put shit on the wall—they are needed by the government and the employers to jail those poverty stricken people they treat like shit. That is why the brutal police and prison guards who ran Iraq for Saddam are back running it for their new masters, cheating the people of the country out of any real regime change.

All of which leads me to conclude that capitalism is the greatest cheat of all.

NO MORE LIES

31 May 2004

Throughout the month of May, a group of Republicans met in Belfast. The purpose of the meetings was to facilitate all Republican ideas, defend the right of people to pursue them free from fear and ensure that the freedom to think is safeguarded. The Republicans surveyed the options available to those intent on promoting Republicanism. As a result the following points were agreed.

Within the Republican family there should be room for the open airing of our disagreements; we cannot move forward until we are able to do so. We believe the criminalisation of Republicanism in the vacuum of the current process is shameful and contrary to the principles of Republicanism. It is our duty to stand up against it and speak out.

It is time for Republicans to reclaim the honour and integrity of the cause which sustained our beliefs; to stand together against the tyranny of abuse and intimidation employed against anyone who has the courage and fortitude to speak out against the wrongs and injustices they see, or suffer themselves.

Republicans should stand with each other in repossessing

the ownership of their struggle. It does not belong to a clique, it is owned by all the people who believe and participate in it.

Republicanism is not about corruption, intimidation, or isolation from one another. It is not self-serving. It is about the Republic, and that Republic is about people. The true spirit of Republicanism is not a cult of personality. It is those who have always been the hidden backbone—once upon a time the volunteer, now the taxi driver, the door man, the day labourer; the support staff in hospitals, waitresses, school workers; the unemployed, marginalised, forgotten.

We have all stood together in times of hardship and crisis. Increasingly we find ourselves standing apart from one another, and our destinies loosened from our grip and out of our control. We once believed we would deliver the Republic to each other where we are equal—Catholic, Protestant and Dissenter.

Today the ideals we fought for are never spoken of, and those who do remember them silenced. Our beliefs were traded for the realities of the current process, a process that suits the interests of political parties and not the common people. These realities include a criminalisation of the people's armies; corruption that fills the coffers of the elite and expands their empires, rather than advances the Republic; children beaten, shot, tortured; comrades isolated, spat upon, silenced, imprisoned, disappeared.

No MORE.

We stand against the tyranny in our midst. It is time to come together, to convene a congress of Republicans, to determine where we are going, to support each other no matter our differences, to reclaim our heritage, integrity and honour, to speak out against injustice, corruption and criminality, and to stand up for the Republic.

Stand with us. Make your voice heard.

Martin Cunningham, *South Down*
Mickey Donnelly, *Derry*
Paddy Fox, *Tyrone*
Tommy Gorman, *Belfast*
Brendan Hughes, *Belfast*
John Kelly, *South Derry*
Anthony McIntyre, *Belfast*
Tommy McKearney, *Monaghan*
Tony McPhilips, *Fermanagh*
Clare Murphy, *Belfast*
Kevin McQuillan, *Belfast*
Francie and Geraldine Perry, *Downpatrick*
Mary Ellen O'Doherty, *Derry*
Fionbarra O'Doctartaigh, *Derry*
Noel O'Reilly, *Belfast*
Liam O Ruairc, *Belfast*
Dolours Price, *Dublin*
Marian Price, *Belfast*
Brendan Shannon, *Belfast*
Róisín Ní Sheanain, *Belfast*
Carrie Twomey, *Belfast*

OUR FENIAN DEAD

29 January 2006

The fools, the fools, the fools, they have left us our Fenian dead. The words were uttered almost a century ago. But today they are still relevant when we watch the behaviour of the hypocritical priests within the Catholic Church. Is it any wonder that you are experiencing the smallest attendance at your chapels? You people hide pervert priests in your midst and then bury them with the blessing of the church. Yet you refuse to allow the body of a dead Republican inside your church. You embrace perverts but reject upright Republicans. Shame.

My uncle Billy died recently. He was a lifelong Republican, a lifelong mass goer and a lifelong decent human being. On his final journey he was shunted from pillar to post because his coffin was covered in the flag of his country. Some priest had exercised the one bit of petty authority left to him and banned the body from entering the chapel. Eventually a Christian priest (not many of them about) was found in Turf Lodge who agreed without hesitation to give my uncle the funeral befitting a man of his beliefs. Father Matt Wallace—who visited Republicans in their sewer of Calcutta, as Cardinal Tomás Ó Fiaich once described the H-Blocks, and who shared his Gallagher's Blues cigarettes with the prisoners gasping for a smoke. Father Matt was the one priest who could be found that was prepared to allow my uncle to enter the chapel.

Uncle Billy was a believer. He was not some imagined communist revolutionary intent on imposing atheism on the people he lived amongst. He believed in Jesus Christ and Irish Republicanism. Not the type of beliefs likely to outlaw Catholicism.

If there is a heaven Billy is in it. The priests can have hell all to themselves. There will hardly be too many tricolour cover coffins going in that direction for them to turn away. The priests need a god to forgive them. Few others will.

DECOMMISSIONED PROVOS THROWN ON THE SCRAP HEAP OF HISTORY

16 April 2006

WRITTEN BY SUZANNE BREEN, *SUNDAY TRIBUNE*

"*Welcome* to my cell," says ex-IRA prisoner, Brendan Hughes, as he opens the door of his tiny, threadbare flat on the Falls Road. "Sometimes, I've sat here crying for a week. I think of all my comrades' suffering and I don't even want to go out. You never really leave prison."

Hughes killed and saw his friends die too. A former "officer commanding" of the Belfast brigade, he's a living legend among Republicans. Small and swarthy with a mop of black hair, he was known as "The Dark."

His bombs reduced the city to rubble; his gun battles with the British entered Republican folklore; he spent 13 years in jail and 53 days on hunger strike. His best friend was Gerry Adams.

Hughes, 57, now lives on disability benefit in Divis Tower - the only part of the flats complex not bulldozed.

Over the past 35 years, around 15,000 Republicans have been imprisoned on both sides of the border. On release, those close to the Sinn Féin leadership usually fare best. A minority secure paid community jobs; the rest are employed in IRA-owned (or supporting) bars and taxi depots.

While some ex-prisoners start businesses independently, the IRA gives others businesses to run. But many former prisoners who—for personal or political reasons—are outside the loop, face greater difficulties.

Last week, an ex-IRA prisoner was one of three men charged in connection with the hijacking of a vodka lorry in Co. Meath. Former security-force members and prison officers received generous retirement and redundancy payments from the state. "We were decommissioned with nothing," says Hughes. "IRA men and women, who gave everything to this struggle, got poverty, premature death, and mental problems in return."

It's the untold story of the Troubles, he claims: "People stay quiet out of loyalty to the movement." Money never mattered to him, he says: "I was offered £50,000 to become an informer. I told them £50m wouldn't sway me. But it's hard to see ex-prisoners destitute when the leadership are so wealthy and have holiday homes."

Hughes mentions Kieran Nugent, the first IRA man on the blanket protest in Long Kesh.

"Kieran died in 2000. They called him a 'river rat' because he spent his last days drinking by the river in Poleglass. Why didn't somebody in the movement not see he'd problems and help him? He was the bravest of the brave. The screws ordered him to wear the prison uniform and he replied, 'You'll have to nail it to my back.'"

Research suggests a third of prisoners suffer broken relationships. Hughes had a baby daughter and his wife was pregnant with their son when he was arrested. "My wife became involved with another man while I was in prison. The lads inside told me to give her a hard time."

"I called her to the jail and told her there was no problem - she was young and deserved a bit of happiness. She always said the war was my number one priority and she was right. I was selfish. I neglected my family. When I got out of jail, I went to her house and shook her partner's hand." Hughes is close to his grown-up daughter but has no relationship with his son.

He was released from prison without skills or qualifications. He began labouring. "A big west Belfast contractor paid us £20 a day. I tried to organise a strike but the other ex-POWs were so desperate, they wouldn't agree. One of the bosses said, 'Brendan, we'll give you £25 a day but don't tell the others.'"

"I told him to stick it up his arse, and I never went back. I wrote an article about it for Republican News but it was heavily censored. People we'd fought for exploited us, and the movement let them." Hughes never considered crime—"I'm not a thief"—but doesn't blame those who do, "so long as they target only big business".

Prison left him with arthritis and weakened his immune system. He's had pneumonia and heart problems, and suffers depression. "After jail, no-one mentioned counselling. I'd to arrange it myself. They say I've post-traumatic stress. The hunger-strikers' faces are always before me."

He speaks of dislocation after jail: "Everything was different. I went for a walk, just to be on my own. The old streets were gone and I got lost in the new streets. A man had to bring me home. Everything was noisy. I hate crowds. I only go to the pub in the afternoon when it's quiet."

Pictures of Che Guevara—laughing, smoking, drinking coffee—dot the living room. "My brother is taking me to Cuba. The revolution improved ordinary people's lives there. It was a waste of time here."

Beneath a picture of the Sacred Heart, is a photo of two tanned, smiling young men in Long Kesh, arms around each other—Hughes and Adams. "I loved Gerry. I don't anymore, but I keep the photos to remind me of the good times."

- - -

Willie Gallagher from Strabane joined the Fianna at 13. Two years later he joined the IRA—"I lied about my age." At 15, he was arrested with a gun. He spent 18 of his next 20 years in jail.

"I don't feel I lost out because I'd no life to lose. I was the youngest in jail and my comrades spoilt me rotten. I remember digging a tunnel for an escape and thinking it a great adventure." By now, Gallagher was with the INLA.

At 20, he embarked on a 50-day hunger-strike after beatings by prison officers: "I lost my eyesight. It took me 18 months to recover. Then, I watched the 10 hunger strikers die. Such brutality damaged me emotionally. I left jail at 25 and wasn't interested in a normal life. I was full of bitterness. There was no point in killing Brits in ones and twos—I wanted to kill lots of them."

"I planted a no-warning bomb in a pub the security forces frequented. Then I went home, got washed and headed into town. Twenty people could have been killed and it wouldn't have fizzed on me." No-one died, but 30 people were injured.

Gallagher went back to jail. His first marriage broke up when he was inside but he remarried within a year of his 1993 release. "My heart never hardened in my personal life, but my reputation means my wife's friends think I'm aggressive. 'Would Willie hit you?' they ask."

Compared to other prisoners, Gallagher, 48, is lucky. His

wife owned her own home—they now have two children—and he secured a paid community job. It's also harder for those who don't come from a Republican family, "but my brothers were involved—two did 10 years—so I'd a lot of support".

He runs a prisoners' group, *Teach na Fáilte*.

Funding has been suspended pending an official investigation amidst allegations of criminality, which the group denies.

Gallagher has been arrested and questioned following a bank robbery in Strabane. The getaway car was bought under the name *Robin Banks*. "I wasn't involved, but if ex-prisoners were, good luck to them. I've no problem with cigarette or alcohol heists either. People who made enormous sacrifices in jail were left with nothing.

"I know one guy who was very fit and always training before he went into jail but he turned to drink and drugs on release and was found dead at 40. If former political prisoners' records were expunged, they'd have far better employment opportunities and life wouldn't be so hard for many." Gallagher has no doubts about his own past: "It's better to fight and lose than not to fight at all."

- - -

Tommy McKearney from the Moy, Co. Tyrone, served 16 years for a UDR man's murder. One of his brothers was shot dead by the SAS, and another brother and an uncle were killed by Loyalists while he was in jail.

"When I got out my father took me to see my brothers' graves. But what struck me was the graves of the post-mistress and the baker. I couldn't believe all the changes in our small community. The world had moved on without me. Many prisoners feel lost for so long."

McKearney now runs Expac, a Monaghan-based group for ex-prisoners in border areas.

"There's no ideal time to go to jail, but it's probably best in your mid-20s. Jail stunts teenagers' emotional development and prison is very hard in your 40s or 50s because you realise how little time is left.

"Serving more than four years affects people. They start to lose contact with the outside world and all but close relatives. After 10, they're institutionalised. It's like marathon runners 'hitting the wall'. After a certain distance, the battle gets too much physically and psychologically."

Ex-prisoners often feel their relatives are strangers and they left their real "family" in jail.

Those who were single when they went to jail then "play catch-up" with children and mortgages in their 40s and 50s, McKearney says. "At retirement time, when life should be easing, they're up to their necks in mortgages and debt."

The situation has improved since the ceasefire, but ex-prisoners still face employment discrimination, he says. They're officially barred from civil-service jobs and unofficially from many others. "How many become teachers or journalists?" McKearney asks. "I mightn't reasonably expect to be able to join the gardaí but I think I should be eligible for a job as local librarian."

Even if ex-prisoners slip through the door, "it's just like with women—there's a glass ceiling."

Neither the Equality Authority nor the North's Equality Commission recognise ex-prisoners as a vulnerable group, he says. "An employer can bin an ex-prisoner's application form, admit it, and the law provides no protection."

Low-paid jobs are no better: "A supermarket can draw up a

list of 20 candidates for shelf-stackers and cashiers. Its head of security, an ex-special branch man, says 'get rid of numbers one and seven.'"

The special branch also visit employers, demanding ex-prisoners are sacked, he says. "I was labouring and they ordered my boss to get rid of me. He told them to get lost, but 99% of employers wouldn't be so principled."

Still, it's easier in border areas than in parts of the country where there's hostility to Republicanism and a smaller black/illegal economy. Exprisoners are usually barred from the US, Canada, Australia and New Zealand, where many would like to begin new lives.

Anthony McIntyre, who served 18 years' imprisonment, says: "I laugh when I hear about an 'IRA pension plan'. The IRA offered me a Christmas loan and nothing else when I was released. I'd two kids and, I'm not ashamed to say, I had to shoplift to feed and clothe them."

Today, Brendan Hughes won't attend any 1916 parade but he'll privately pay tribute at the IRA Belfast brigade monument. "I keep wondering 'what was it all about?'" he says. "The doctors tell me not to drink but I do. It eases the pain, it doesn't kill it."

A picture of the hunger strikers hangs in Hughes's hallway. "Soldiers of our past, heroes of our future," it says. Somehow, it doesn't seem that way.

O'RAW TOLD ME HIS CONCERNS

19 May 2006

It is not my intention to take sides in the ongoing debate over the claims made in the book *Blanketmen* by its author Richard O'Rawe.

I am not in a position to speak authoritatively on the matter.

I was in the same block as Richard O'Rawe at the time of the events he refers to but not on the same wing.

However, there has been some attempt to present O'Rawe as a person who made no effort to tell any former prisoner of his suspicions over a 24-year period. This is simply not so.

I am a former prisoner whom O'Rawe talked to on a number of occasions about the things that concerned him and which eventually appeared in his book.

I can also state I am not the only former prisoner O'Rawe has raised the matter with.

BRENDAN HUGHES
Former OC of the H-Block Blanket Men
Belfast

RISKING THE LIVES OF VOLUNTEERS IS NOT THE IRA WAY

13 July 2006

IRISH NEWS

In a recent BBC documentary Bernadette McAliskey (née Devlin) stated that she would have let Sean McKenna die during the 1980 hunger strike in order to outmanoeuvre British brinkmanship. Implicit in her comments was a criticism of those senior Republicans who decided against pursuing the option favoured by Bernadette. As the IRA leader in charge of that hunger strike I had given Sean McKenna a guarantee that were he to lapse into a coma I would not permit him to die.

When the awful moment arrived I kept my word to him. Having made that promise, to renege on it once Sean had reached a point where he was no longer capable of making a decision for himself, I would have been guilty of his murder. Whatever the strategic merits of Bernadette's favoured option, they are vastly outweighed by ethical considerations.

There are terrible things that happen in the course of any war. Those of us who feel obliged to fight wars must take responsibility for the terrible consequences of the actions that we initiate. I can live with that. In war we kill enemies and expect to be killed by them. I can stand over the military decisions that I made during our war against the British. But there are no circumstances in which I was prepared to make a cynical decision that would have manipulated events to the point where a Republican comrade would forfeit his life.

25 years on, I have no reason to change my mind that the decision I made to save the life of Sean McKenna was the proper one. Faced with similar circumstances I would do the same again. History may judge my actions differently, but preventing Sean McKenna from becoming history, rather than my own place in history, was my prevailing concern.

HUNGER STRIKER IN FIGHT FOR SIGHT

October 2006

ALLISON MORRIS, *IRISH NEWS*

The leader of the IRA prisoners in the Maze in 1980 has undergone an operation to save his sight, badly damaged by 52 days of starvation during the first Hunger Strike.

Brendan "The Dark" Hughes underwent a cataract operation on Wednesday to save the sight in his left eye.

He will have to undergo a second operation in two months to restore sight to his right eye.

Doctors have told the former Republican prisoner that his eyesight has been badly damaged due to the time he spent on hunger strike while a prisoner.

Speaking from his home in Divis Tower in west Belfast the 58-year-old said the lasting mental and physical effects of the prison protests are the true untold legacy of the time.

"I'm not unique, there are hundreds of men out there carrying around problems from that time," he said.

"If not physical problems there are men with mental prob-

lems, alcohol problems, depression, trouble holding down a job
or a relationship.

"The lead up to the Hunger Strikes was well documented we
were brutalised, our food was urinated on we were beaten and
tortured.

"It came to a point where men were coming off the protest
because they just couldn't take any more, it was considered our
last option.

"I led the first hunger strike and was also responsible for
calling it off, I've been criticised for that by certain people but
if the truth be told, and I have never said this before, not one
of those men was prepared to die.

"Before Sean McKenna went into a coma he said to me,
'Dark don't let me die' and I promised him I wouldn't.

"They were putting him onto a stretcher to take him to the
hospital, we thought an agreement was on the table and I just
shouted up the corridor, 'feed him' and with those two words
the first hunger strike was over.

"I weighed about five stone at the time, you could smell the
rotting bodies in the hospital ward, I was very conscious of the
smell of my own body eating itself.

"The doctor told the orderlies to feed us scrambled egg and
toast, you'd think you wouldn't be able to eat after all that time
but you can and so that's what we ate; scrambled egg."

The men were kept in the prison hospital until they had
gained enough weight to be returned to the H-Blocks.

Hughes says that almost immediately he noticed a problem
with his sight and went from having perfect vision to needing
glasses. "During hunger strike you notice first your sense of
smell and taste go, then your vision, my sight suffered and that
has been degenerative.

"About 18 months ago my vision became badly blurred, like a spiders web over your eyes I was lucky to get a cancellation for the cataract surgery this week and so that's one eye done, hopefully it was successful.

"I've also got arthritis and chest problems but it is the mental problems that are the most debilitating.

"I've never been able to settle, I don't like being around crowds of people.

"The only reason I think I settled in Divis Tower is because it's quite cellular, I suppose that's what I respond to."

Strongly opposed to the second hunger strike Hughes says he feels many ex-prisoners have not been given enough help to adjust following their release from prison.

Released from prison in 1986 having served just over 13 years in jail, he says he has struggled with life on the outside and at times turned to alcohol.

"I argued strongly against the second hunger strike but by then I was no longer OC, I was just an ordinary volunteer. Bobby [Sands] knew he would die but he thought his own death would be enough to force the Brits into a settlement, we know now that was not to be the case and 10 men were to lose their lives.

"There are men still suffering in silence today, the recent commemoration events to mark the 25 anniversary of the Hunger Strike didn't even touch on that terrible legacy.

"Ex-prisoners groups are fine as long as you conform to the present political situation—if you voice dissent then you're cast aside.

"They are not doing enough because they are too selective as to who they'll help.

"Painting murals on walls to commemorate blanketmen after they have died a slow and lonely death from alcohol abuse is no use to anyone.

"I would hate for young people now to have this romanticised versions of the events of that time and what went on in the prison, the truth is so very far removed from that and I suppose I'm living proof of that."

SINN FÉIN TRYING TO SMEAR
"DISSENTERS"

3 January 2007

BRENDAN HUGHES AND JOHN KELLY, *IRISH NEWS*

A number of years ago a body of Republicans came together in support of open debate and an end to a range of sordid practices that had brought Republicanism into disrepute. The group, while loosely referring to itself as a congress, came to be known as *No More Lies*.

It aspired to offer some form of moral protection to those Republicans who felt they wanted to push back the party censors and thought police.

Today it seems that the need to refute lies and offer moral protection is as great as it was then.

Of particular concern are certain allegations being peddled by the Sinn Féin leadership.

Supported by the PSNI, it claims to be under physical threat from some people opposed to its partitionist policies and its eagerness to embrace the PSNI.

In our view there are threats being made. But they are coming from Sinn Féin and are directed against Republicans who seek a wider debate on the policing matter.

A number of people have been warned by Sinn Féin that they must not attend independent meetings organised by Republicans around the policing issue.

It is not the threat of physical attack that Sinn Féin leaders fear.

This is evident from the way they continue to go about their daily lives. It is the possibility of Republicans fed up with Sinn Féin lies and deceit deciding to mount an electoral challenge that sends shudders of anxiety through the leadership circles. We have no position on electoral intervention one way or the other. We do not know if any electoral challenge has been discussed. But those who wish to discuss all matters relevant to Republicanism—including an alternative electoral strategy to Sinn Féin's, must be both free and safe to do so. We are concerned that in a bid to stifle wider discussion within the Republican community, Sinn Féin is pursuing a strategy of threat against dissenting voices. They are disguising their own menace by attributing violent intent to those voices. Such voices are healthy in a Republicanism unafraid of critical self-examination. They must be protected against Sinn Féin leadership threats and smears used to undermine their credibility.

Let the debate take place and the most honest participants win.

Under no circumstances should it be prevented from happening.

Afterword

ESSAY FROM D. ÓG
"25 YEARS OF GOT FUCK ALL"
2023 April

D. Óg was born of the generation often referred to as the Good Friday Generation. He is an independent Socialist Republican from Dublin—born to a Republican family. His grandfather instilled in him a love of the Irish language, An Ghaeilge. Óg's grandfather was a native speaker of the language and often remarked that he felt much more comfortable conversing in Irish than English. As well as the language his grandfather instilled in him a love of Ireland, her hills and valleys, her music and song, her national sports of hurling and Gaelic football, and her centuries long struggle for freedom. Though Óg's grandfather was involved in the struggle to free the North of Ireland, he never spoke about it. It was only at his grandfather's funeral when a guard of honour lined the church gates that Óg found out.

For Óg, Irish Republicanism runs in his veins—whenever he goes to a commemoration or event, he often thinks not only of those they are commemorating, but all those brave volunteers, those who devoted their lives to the cause of Ireland. Brendan Hughes is someone Óg immensely admires.

This year marks 25 years since the signing of the Good Friday Agreement, and the leadership of the Republican Movement selling out the struggle to assume their place at the table of the oppressor. The period of time from 1969-1998 is often referred to as *The Troubles*, however it should be referred to as a war, and it was only the latest period of an 800 years long struggle for the Irish people to achieve national liberation.

Much will be written about the life and struggle of Brendan Hughes, so it need not be said again here. However, it must be said that Brendan became outspoken against the leadership of the Irish Republican Army and Sinn Féin at a time when it was very unpopular to do so. His criticism stems from the fact that a war had been fought for 30 years and the army had remained undefeated and succeeded in bringing the most powerful army on earth to the negotiating table, but had sold out the men, women, and children who had sacrificed everything so they could be offered a chance to rule on behalf of Britain in their colonial parliament of Stormont.

Throughout history, whenever a colonial power could not defeat a people's resistance on the battlefield, they choose certain malevolent figures who are only out for personal gain to exploit, and this is what occurred in Ireland with the Republican leadership. Hughes quickly identified the issues with the leadership and earnestly spoke out against them, calling them the "Armani Suit Brigade" and criticised their meetings at high end Belfast hotels while the nationalist community, mere miles away, were suffering from some of the worst poverty in Europe. The Republican movement went from challenging the might of the British Empire, even striking in London, in the Belly of the Beast, in their economic warfare campaign, to surrendering and giving up their weapons at the behest of a leadership who cared naught for the brave volunteers who put their lives on the line, or the community they claimed to represent.

Hughes, in writing on the signing of the peace agreement some years after the fact, referred to it as the *Got Fuck All Agreement*. Nothing of value had been gained. Britain remained, and still remains in control of 6 out of 32 of Ireland's counties, where some 10,000 armed British soldiers patrol the streets of the North of Ireland. The difference between Ireland in 1998, before the peace agreement, and now in 2023 is that we have undergone a sinister normalization campaign of the British occupation. Every bourgeois political party rolled out the red carpet for Bill Clinton, and for the British to enforce a treaty upon us which copper-fastened Britain's rule in Ireland. To speak out against this was to be in favour of violence or worse, a supporter of terrorism. "The time for the gun has left Irish politics," we were told, and now was "the time for peace, but pay no heed to the thousands of British soldiers, and the reformed RUC, Britain's armed police who terrorize nationalist areas daily, and subject Irish people to nearly twice as many stop and searches as Protestants."

To have spoken out against this betrayal and normalization process would have meant you were dubbed a "dissident Republican" by the media, and also by now constitutional nationalists (former Republicans now in power sharing). The meaning behind this term is ironic as it implies that those who continue to advocate for resistance to British rule in Ireland have deviated from Republicanism. It was not Brendan Hughes nor those who still call out the sell outs who rule on Britain's behalf who have deviated from Republicanism. But, rather than see this term as an insult, Hughes embraced and referred to himself as "an unrepentant Fenian bastard."

This year, 25 years on from the signing of the GFA, we will hear many bourgeois parties refer to the lead up to and aftermath of the signing as the peace process. We must confront this narrative as Brendan did and ask, *what peace*? What is peaceful about families having their mothers and fathers dragged away by police in the dead of night? What is peaceful about young men and women taking their own lives because they will never have a chance to have a place to call their own because the cost of living is too high? What is peaceful about 10,000 armed soldiers enforcing Britain's occupation of Ireland? There is no peace in Ireland despite the media and ruling class shoving the narrative of such down our throats. For us, we live everyday of our lives through occupation and class warfare designed to fatten the pockets of the ruling class. For us who were born just before and after the peace agreement, we are often referred to as the Good Friday Generation, it would be more apt to refer to us as the *Got Fuck All Generation* as we have lived through the constant cycle of boom and bust, and the sharpening contradictions of capitalism.

Just as Brendan, we must continue to speak out, however unpopular, against the ongoing normalization of the so-called peace process. We must continue to rebuild a revolutionary movement, which is lacking after the disintegration of the Republican movement. And we must continue the unfinished struggle of our ancestors, who smashed the Vikings at Clontarf in 1014, who massacred the English lords at Glenmalure in 1580, who littered the streets around Mount Street Bridge with the bodies of British soldiers in 1916, and who, being deprived of any other weapon in the concentration camps of Long Kesh in 1981 decided to use their bodies to show the British they were not defeated. We must remain true to the Republic and honour Brendan Hughes's memory by fulfilling the cause for which he sacrificed so much.

Just as the mortally wounded Cú Chulainn refused to die lying down, and bound himself to a tree, succumbing to his wounds warrior like with his sword in his hand, The Dark refused similarly. Although scarred in body and mind from years of torture in Britain's concentration camps, he stood true to the Republic and refused to sell out. He remained unbowed, unbroken, and the name of *The Dark* will live on in the hearts of all those who believe in a 32-county Socialist Republic forever.